BIBLE WORDS CROSSWORD PUZZLES 4

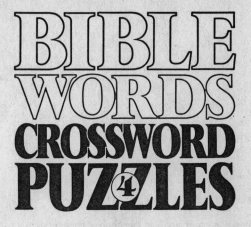

BIBLE WORDS CROSSWORD PUZZLES 4

MARVIN KANANEN

BAKER BOOK HOUSE
Grand Rapids, Michigan 49516

ISBN: 0-8010-5296-3

Printed in the United States of America

The King James Version of the Bible has been used to prepare most of the puzzle clues. Other versions used are Living Bible (LB), New International Version (NIV), New American Standard Bible (NASB), New King James Version (NKJV), and Good News Bible (GNB).

The fifty crossword puzzles
in this book are purposely designed
to help the users uncover Bible truths
as they solve the puzzle clues.
Most of the clues
are based on Scripture references.
Solutions are placed
at the back of the book.
Happy puzzling!

1

Across

1. He planteth an ____, and the rain doth nourish it. (Isa. 44:14)
4. Rate (Latin).
8. And wiped his feet with her ____. (John 12:3)
12. Caviar.
13. The children of ____ which were in Telassar. (Isa. 37:12)
14. Noun suffix.
15. Greek goddess of healing.
16. No man could learn that ____. (Rev. 14:3)
17. Heareth the word, and ____ with joy receiveth it. (Matt. 13:20)
18. The inhabitants of the earth will ____ over them. (Rev. 11:10 NIV)
20. The ____ of the Lord must not strive. (2 Tim. 2:24)
22. Last of all the woman ____ also. (Luke 20:32)
24. It was impossible for God to ____. (Heb. 6:18)
25. ____ thought she had been drunken. (1 Sam. 1:13)
27. Neither ____ we eat any man's bread for nought. (2 Thess. 3:8)
29. When the devil had ____ all the temptation. (Luke 4:13)
33. Rosary piece.
35. God hath said, Ye shall not ____ of it. (Gen. 3:3)
37. ____ obeyed Abraham, calling him lord. (1 Peter 3:6)
38. Iraqi port.
40. The land of ____, on the east of Eden. (Gen. 4:16)
42. Below the ____, gourds encircled it. (1 Kings 7:24 NIV)
43. The sons of Caleb the son of Jephunneh; ____, Elah, and Naam. (1 Chron. 4:15)
45. I will go to its highest ____. (Isa. 37:24 NASB)
47. Unvarying.
51. ____ had sent him bound unto Caiaphas. (John 18:24)
54. Darkness is ____, and the true light now shineth. (1 John 2:8)
55. Slew of the Philistines six hundred men with an ox ____. (Judg. 3:31)
57. Sir, come down ere my child die. (John 4:49)
58. As he saith also in ____, I will call them my people. (Rom. 9:25)
59. He that doeth ____ hath not seen God. (3 John 11)
60. Ye ____ then how that by works a man is justified. (James 2:24)
61. Then Mary took about a pint of pure ____. (John 12:3 NIV)
62. But in works they ____ him. (Titus 1:16)
63. Be not as the hypocrites, of a ____ countenance. (Matt. 6:16)

Down

1. Sand expanses.
2. Still other seed fell on good ____. (Matt. 13:8 NIV)
3. ____ had a quarrel against him [the Baptist]. (Mark 6:19)
4. ____ the sabbath day according to the commandment. (Luke 23:56)
5. Why make ye this ____, and weep? (Mark 5:39)
6. Captains over fifties, and captains over ____. (Deut. 1:15)
7. For Satan himself is transformed into an ____ of light. (2 Cor. 11:14)
8. By the word of God the ____ were of old. (2 Peter 3:5)
9. ____, a prophetess, the daughter of Phanuel. (Luke 2:36)
10. Religious image.
11. The veil of the temple was ____ in twain. (Mark 15:38)
19. Howl, O Heshbon, for ____ is spoiled. (Jer. 49:3)
21. The wheat and the ____ were not smitten. (Exod. 9:32)
23. Ye are in our hearts to ____ and live with you. (2 Cor. 7:3)
25. Their lives ____ away in their mothers' arms. (Lam. 2:12 NIV)
26. Pasture.

Grid numbers: 1, 2, 3, 4, 5, 6, 7, 8, 9, 10, 11, 12, 13, 14, 15, 16, 17, 18, 19, 20, 21, 22, 23, 24, 25, 26, 27, 28, 29, 30, 31, 32, 33, 34, 35, 36, 37, 38, 39, 40, 41, 42, 43, 44, 45, 46, 47, 48, 49, 50, 51, 52, 53, 54, 55, 56, 57, 58, 59, 60, 61, 62, 63

28. Ahisamach, of the tribe of ____, an engraver. (Exod. 38:23)

30. There fell on him a mist and a ____. (Acts 13:11)

31. Of ____, the family of the Erites. (Num. 26:16)

32. Thou shalt in any wise let the ____ go. (Deut. 22:7)

34. The boat ____ on the surface. (Gen. 7:18 GNB)

36. The coat was without seam, woven from the ____. (John 19:23)

39. Nigerian native.

41. It is an unruly evil, full of ____ poison. (James 3:8)

44. They ____ him till he was ashamed. (2 Kings 2:17)

46. If any man sin, we have ____ advocate. (1 John 2:1)

47. Are built ____ the foundation of the apostles. (Eph. 2:20)

48. U.S. space agency.

49. Elbe tributary

50. For in him we live, and ____, and have our being. (Acts 17:28)

52. He has brought Greeks into the temple ____. (Acts 21:28 NIV)

53. In Isaac shall thy ____ be called. (Heb. 11:18)

56. Their villages were, Etam, and ____. (1 Chron. 4:32)

2

Across

1. Balaam smote the ____, to turn her. (Num. 22:23)
4. This time will I come, and ____ shall have a son. (Rom. 9:9)
9. He planteth an ____, and the rain doth nourish it. (Isa. 44:14)
12. River (Spanish).
13. Faith, if it hath not works, is dead, being ____. (James 2:17)
14. Tribute to whom tribute is ____. (Rom. 13:7)
15. Which of you by taking thought can ____ one cubit unto his stature? (Matt. 6:27)
16. Thou art wretched, and miserable, and poor, and blind, and ____. (Rev. 3:17)
17. Jephunneh, and Pispah, and ____. (1 Chron. 7:38)
18. Cretians are alway liars, evil ____, slow bellies. (Titus 1:12)
20. Gambled.
22. Woe ____ that man by whom the Son of man is betrayed! (Mark 14:21)
23. In Isaac shall thy ____ be called. (Heb. 11:18)
25. The twelfth month, that is, the month ____. (Esther 3:7)
28. We ____ the sentence of death in ourselves. (2 Cor. 1:9)
29. They resolved to drive the ship ____ it if they could. (Acts 27:39 NASB)
33. ____ obeyed Abraham, calling him lord. (1 Peter 3:6)
34. Stand in ____, and sin not. (Ps. 4:4)
35. They gnawed their tongues for ____. (Rev. 16:10)
36. I am alive for evermore, ____. (Rev.1:18)
37. She called his name ____-oni: but his father called him Benjamin. (Gen. 35:18)
38. Every ____ is known by his own fruit. (Luke 6:44)
39. We are ____, when we are weak. (2 Cor. 13:9)
41. Direction: Joppa to Lydda (10 miles).
42. ____ with thine adversary quickly. (Matt. 5:25)

45. A door of utterance, to speak the mystery of ____. (Col. 4:3)
49. Is any thing ____ hard for the LORD? (Gen. 18:14)
50. ____ had waited till Job had spoken. (Job 32:4)
53. I ____ my knees unto the Father. (Eph. 3:14)
54. Shamed, who built ____, and Lod. (1 Chron. 8:12)
55. Book of Mohammed.
56. Uzzi, Uzziel, and Jerimoth, and ____, five. (1 Chron. 7:7)
57. Can you make a ____ of him like a bird? (Job 41:5 NIV)
58. Wandering ____, to whom is reserved the blackness. (Jude 13)
59. Ye shall have tribulation ____ days. (Rev. 2:10)

Down

1. ____, and Dumah, and Eshean. (Josh. 15:52)
2. He smote Peter on the ____, and raised him up. (Acts 12:7)
3. Although you wash yourself with ____. (Jer. 2:22 NIV)
4. Holy (Spanish).
5. ____ that great city Babylon that mighty city! (Rev. 18:10)
6. Korean soldier.
7. Donkey (French).
8. The way of the slothful man is as an ____ of thorns. (Prov. 15:19)
9. He separated the sons of ____, he set the bounds. (Deut. 32:8)
10. We are ____ that the judgment of God is according to truth. (Rom. 2:2)
11. The ____ of the woman is the man. (1 Cor. 11:3)
19. Saying, We have seen ____ things to day. (Luke 5:26)
21. One who takes in another's child.
23. Stones, ____ with saws, within and without. (1 Kings 7:9)
24. A river went out of ____ to water the garden. (Gen. 2:10)

25. Maachah the mother of ____ the king. (2 Chron. 15:16)
26. It shall be seven days under the ____. (Lev. 22:27)
27. All seek their own, not the things which ____ Jesus Christ's. (Phil. 2:21)
28. Bean (Spanish).
30. Near (Scottish).
31. ____ the kine to the cart, and bring their calves. (1 Sam. 6:7)
32. Finally, be ye all of ____ mind. (1 Peter 3:8)
40. And the ____, and the onions, and the garlick. (Num. 11:5)
41. Whoever ____ evil becomes a prey. (Isa. 59:15 NIV)
42. Above.

43. They have ____ in the way of Cain. (Jude 11)
44. The love of money is the ____ of all evil. (1 Tim. 6:10)
45. To scorch.
46. Philippine lizard.
47. For he is lunatick, and ____ vexed. (Matt. 17:15)
48. The figurehead of the ____ gods Castor and Pollux. (Acts 28:11 NIV)
51. They took ____, Abram's brother's son. (Gen. 14:12)
52. ____ the son of Ikkesh the Tekoite. (1 Chron. 27:9)

9

3

Across

1. The darkness is ____, and the true light now shineth. (1 John 2:8)
5. But Christ as a son ____ his own house. (Heb. 3:6)
9. The poor man had nothing, save one little ____ lamb. (2 Sam. 12:3)
12. The burning ____, that shall consume the eyes. (Lev. 26:16)
13. Those that were clean escaped from them who ____ in error. (2 Peter 2:18)
14. Consider what I ____; and the Lord give thee understanding. (2 Tim. 2:7)
15. Noah, being warned of God of things not ____ as yet. (Heb. 11:7)
16. The Spirit searcheth all things, yea, the ____ things of God. (1 Cor. 2:10)
17. How long will it be ____ thou be quiet? (Jer. 47:6)
18. The ____ of cattle are perplexed. (Joel 1:18)
20. The ships were ____ and were not able to set sail to trade. (2 Chron. 20:37 NIV)
22. Time period.
24. Extol Him who rides on the clouds, By His name ____. (Ps. 68:4 NKJV)
25. ____, make this man to understand the vision. (Dan. 8:16)
29. The sins of others ____ behind them. (1 Tim. 5:24 NIV)
33. Debate.
34. The wheat and the ____ were not smitten. (Exod. 9:32)
36. Ye should earnestly contend for the faith which was ____ delivered unto the saints. (Jude 3)
37. As the waters that are poured down a ____ place. (Mic. 1:4)
39. I have ____, Apollos watered. (1 Cor. 3:6)
41. Jacob ____ pottage; and Esau came from the field. (Gen. 25:29)
43. The sons of Bela; Ezbon, and Uzzi, Uzziel, and Jerimoth, and ____, five. (1 Chron. 7:7)
44. He shewed himself alive after his ____. (Acts 1:3)
48. Did not ____ the son of Zerah commit a trespass. (Josh. 22:20)

52. He searches the farthest recesses for ____ in the blackest darkness. (Job 28:3 NIV)
53. No one ____ righteously and no one pleads. (Isa. 59:4 NASB)
55. He that loveth his life shall ____ it. (John 12:25)
56. He is lodged in the house of one Simon a tanner by the ____ side. (Acts 10:32)
57. Bone (Greek).
58. Repent; or ____ I will come unto thee quickly. (Rev. 2:16)
59. To him that overcometh will I give to ____ of the hidden manna. (Rev. 2:17)
60. Thou set thy ____ among the stars. (Obad. 4)
61. If ye be Christ's, then are ye Abraham's ____. (Gal. 3:29)

Down

1. To smash.
2. Shammah the son of ____ the Hararite. (2 Sam. 23:11)
3. Litigant.
4. Set the sole of her foot upon the ground for delicateness and ____. (Deut. 28:56)
5. The ____ commandment is the word which ye have heard from the beginning. (1 John 2:7)
6. The prophets went, and stood to ____ afar off. (2 Kings 2:7)
7. Let ____ man be swift to hear, slow to speak. (James 1:19)
8. I ____: Let no one take me for a fool. (2 Cor. 11:16 NIV)
9. He called the name of the well ____. (Gen. 26:20)
10. Be thou ____ also; for he hath greatly withstood our words. (2 Tim. 4:15)
11. Leah was tender ____; but Rachel was beautiful. (Gen. 29:17)
19. ____ Lanka.
21. He commanded to bring the book of records of the ____. (Esther 6:1)
23. Chalice veil.
25. Petrol.

26. Agent (abbrev.).
27. Bough (obs.).
28. The ____ of truth shall be established for ever. (Prov. 12:19)
30. Go to the ____, thou sluggard; consider her ways. (Prov. 6:6)
31. Out of whose womb came the ____? (Job 38:29)
32. He ____ captivity captive. (Eph. 4:8)
35. Therefore ____ thought she had been drunken. (1 Sam. 1:13)
38. The ____ of asps is under their lips. (Rom. 3:13)
40. Jephunneh, and Pispah, and ____. (1 Chron. 7:38)
42. Extinguish.

44. ____ your riddle, that we may hear it. (Judg. 14:13 NKJV)
45. Jesus entered the temple ____ and began driving out those who were buying and selling. (Mark 11:15 NIV)
46. The fifth angel poured out his vial upon the ____ of the beast. (Rev. 16:10)
47. They straightway left their ____, and followed him. (Matt. 4:20)
49. Look unto the rock whence ye are hewn, and to the ____ of the pit. (Isa. 51:1)
50. Hartebeeste.
51. For ye have ____ of patience. (Heb. 10:36)
54. Our brother Timothy is ____ at liberty. (Heb. 13:23)

11

4

Across

1. Cain talked with ____ his brother. (Gen. 4:8)
5. Hear this word, you ____ of Bashan. (Amos 4:1 NIV)
9. I knew a man in Christ above fourteen years ____. (2 Cor. 12:2)
12. What things ____ gain to me, those I counted loss. (Phil. 3:7)
13. Wet.
14. The rich, in that he is made ____. (James 1:10)
15. Punish the men that are settled on their ____. (Zeph. 1:12)
16. Deceiveth his own heart, this man's ____ is vain. (James 1:26)
18. There fell a noisome and grievous ____ upon the men. (Rev. 16:2)
20. Tears.
21. Philippi, which is the chief city of that part of Macedonia, and a ____. (Acts 16:12)
24. To ____, that God was in Christ. (2 Cor. 5:19)
25. Are not ____ and Pharpar, rivers of Damascus? (2 Kings 5:12)
26. Your lightning ____ up the world. (Ps. 77:18 NIV)
27. Uz, and ____, and Gether, and Mash. (Gen. 10:23)
30. No one ____ it aside or adds conditions to it. (Gal. 3:15 NASB)
31. A brother offended is harder to be ____. (Prov. 18:19)
32. Or clothe his neck with a flowing ____. (Job 39:19 NIV)
33. He cometh with clouds; and every ____ shall see him. (Rev. 1:7)
34. On the morrow I ____ on the judgment seat. (Acts 25:17)
35. The wicked man ____ deceptive wages. (Prov. 11:18 NIV)
36. The flesh sets ____ desire against the Spirit. (Gal. 5:17 NASB)
37. Thou hast a few names even in ____. (Rev. 3:4)
38. Call me blessed: and she called his name ____. (Gen. 30:13)
41. Whose waters cast up mire and ____. (Isa. 57:20)
42. A ____, named Gamaliel, a doctor of the law. (Acts 5:34)
44. We know that an ____ is nothing in the world. (1 Cor. 8:4)
48. He had by himself purged ____ sins. (Heb. 1:3)
49. Fear God. Honour the ____. (1 Peter 2:17)
50. Moses set out with Joshua his ____. (Exod. 24:13 NIV)
51. Thou shalt in any wise let the ____ go. (Deut. 22:7)
52. Take thine ____, eat, drink, and be merry. (Luke 12:19)
53. Ye ____ men with burdens grievous to be borne. (Luke 11:46)

Down

1. Pierce his ear with an ____. (Exod. 21:6 NIV)
2. And for the ____ that is in the land of Assyria. (Isa. 7:18)
3. How long will it be ____ they attain to innocency? (Hos. 8:5)
4. You still need someone to teach you the first ____ of God's message. (Heb. 5:12 GNB)
5. ____ neither purse, nor scrip, nor shoes. (Luke 10:4)
6. As he saith also in ____, I will call them my people, which were not my people. (Rom. 9:25)
7. Will (obsolete).
8. Themselves, sensual, having not the ____. (Jude 19)
9. Icelandic distance measure.
10. There is none ____ but one, that is, God. (Mark 10:18)
11. A slave, although he ____ the whole estate. (Gal. 4:1 NIV)
17. ____ thee hence, Satan: for it is written, Thou shalt worship the Lord thy God. (Matt. 4:10)
19. Fuegan Indian.
21. Ye shall in no ____ enter into the kingdom. (Matt. 5:20)
22. What shall the end be of them that ____ not the gospel of God? (1 Peter 4:17)
23. The Jews of ____ sought to stone thee. (John 11:8)

24. Encamped against the fenced cities, and thought to ____ them for himself. (2 Chron. 32:1)

26. Rest, and stand in thy ____ at the end of the days. (Dan. 12:13)

27. We have many things to say, and ___ to be uttered. (Heb. 5:11)

28. ____, Eliab, and Benaiah, and Maaseiah. (1 Chron. 15:18)

29. The more abundantly I love you, the ____ I be loved. (2 Cor. 12:15)

31. A servant, and ____ made in the likeness of men. (Phil. 2:7)

32. The sons of Israel went up in ____ array. (Exod. 13:18 NASB)

34. The servants did ____ him with the palms. (Mark 14:65)

35. First the blade, then the ____. (Mark 4:28)

36. Comparative suffix.

37. God hath given thee, in the ____, and in the straitness. (Deut. 28:53)

38. Footless.

39. Three were born unto him of the daughter of ____ the Canaanitess. (1 Chron. 2:3)

40. Do thyself no ____: for we are all here. (Acts 16:28)

41. Hid themselves in the ____ and in the rocks. (Rev. 6:15)

43. The children of Keros, the children of ____. (Neh. 7:47)

45. Geometric abbreviation.

46. The ____ number of them is to be redeemed. (Num. 3:48)

47. We passed to the ____ of a small island called Cauda. (Acts 27:16 NIV)

5

Across

1. Bashemath the daughter of ____ the Hittite. (Gen. 26:34)
5. The dumb ____ speaking with man's voice. (2 Peter 2:16)
8. Observe the month of ____, and keep the passover. (Deut. 16:1)
12. Napoleon's 1796 Italian victory site.
13. The wheat and the ____ were not smitten. (Exod. 9:32)
14. All the depths of the ____ will dry up. (Zech. 10:11 NASB)
15. As ____ as I had eaten it, my belly was bitter. (Rev. 10:10)
16. Pursued the Philistines, and smote them, until they came under Beth-____. (1 Sam. 7:11)
17. Narrow opening.
18. They crucify to themselves the Son of God ____. (Heb. 6:6)
20. Cursed be the deceiver, which . . . ____, and sacrificeth unto the Lord a corrupt thing. (Mal. 1:14)
22. Are ye now made perfect by ____ flesh? (Gal. 3:3)
23. What mean these seven ____ lambs? (Gen. 21:29)
24. Bring Zenas the ____ and Apollos on their journey. (Titus 3:13)
27. They shall ____ every strong hold. (Hab. 1:10)
31. Of ____, the family of the Erites. (Num. 26:16)
32. Ye did ____ well; who did hinder you? (Gal. 5:7)
33. Courting.
37. Ye ___ the Holy One and the Just. (Acts 3:14)
40. ____, give me this water, that I thirst not. (John 4:15)
41. Many deceivers ____ entered into the world. (2 John 7)
42. And all the ____ of the children of Israel. (Acts 5:21)
45. Cut off from Babylon the name, and remnant, and son, and ____, saith the LORD. (Isa. 14:22)
49. ____, lama sabachthani? (Mark 15:34)
50. Samuel feared to shew ____ the vision. (1 Sam. 3:15)
52. The ____, and the coney: for they chew the cud. (Deut. 14:7)
53. Icelandic length.
54. French place of business.
55. ____ were your children unclean. (1 Cor. 7:14)
56. Oriental nurse.
57. Snake-like fish.
58. European kite.

Down

1. Fraulien's name.
2. Sponge gourd.
3. There is a bad ____, for he has been there four days. (John 11:39 NIV)
4. The ____ and nine which went not astray. (Matt. 18:13)
5. Against him that bendeth let the ____ bend his bow. (Jer. 51:3)
6. The children of ____, the children of Padon. (Neh. 7:47)
7. Worshipped and ____ the creature more than the Creator. (Rom. 1:25)
8. Give an ____ to every man that asketh you. (1 Peter 3:15)
9. Gall.
10. Island.
11. In his days did Hiel the ____-elite build Jericho. (1 Kings 16:34)
19. ____ of her penury hath cast in all the living. (Luke 21:4)
21. ____ no man any thing, but to love one another. (Rom. 13:8)
24. Paul was to be ____ into the castle. (Acts 21:37)
25. Jephunneh, and Pispah, and ____. (1 Chron. 7:38)

Crossword Grid

1	2	3	4		5	6	7		8	9	10	11
12					13				14			
15					16				17			
18			19				20	21				
		22					23					
24	25	26					27			28	29	30
31										32		
33			34	35	36		37	38	39			
		40					41					
42	43	44				45			46	47	48	
49				50	51		52					
53				54			55					
56				57			58					

26. We do you to ____ of the grace of God. (2 Cor. 8:1)

28. And ____, five; heads of the house. (1 Chron. 7:7)

29. That he may exalt you in ____ time. (1 Peter 5:6)

30. The ____ of all things is at hand. (1 Peter 4:7)

34. The prophet ____ the son of Amoz, prayed and cried to heaven. (2 Chron. 32:20)

35. Louse egg.

36. Had given them much exhortation, he came into ____. (Acts 20:2)

37. The second ____, of Abigail the Carmelitess. (1 Chron. 3:1)

38. Sir, come down ____ my child die. (John 4:49)

39. The sons of Izhar; Korah, and ____; and Zichri. (Exod. 6:21)

42. Send ye the lamb to the ruler of the land from ____. (Isa. 16:1)

43. In ____ were twelve fountains of water. (Num. 33:9)

44. Woman's name.

46. He commanded him to be kept in Herod's judgment ____. (Acts 23:35)

47. Gaelic.

48. They will ____ out of his kingdom everything that causes sin. (Matt. 13:41 NIV)

51. Eternal life, which God, that cannot ____, promised. (Titus 1:2)

6

Across

1. The LORD shall ____ to me another son. (Gen. 30:24)
4. See what they ____ from their mouths. (Ps. 59:7 NIV)
8. "Come, I will ____ you the bride." (Rev. 21:9 NIV)
12. Hath Satan filled thine heart to ____? (Acts 5:3)
13. Man, take thee a ____, and lay it before thee. (Ezek. 4:1)
14. The devil threw him down, and ____ him. (Luke 9:42)
15. Jephunneh, and Pispah, and ____. (1 Chron. 7:38)
16. The ____ of the dead lived not again. (Rev. 20:5)
17. The unlearned say ____ at thy giving of thanks. (1 Cor. 14:16)
18. That could not make him that did the ____ perfect. (Heb. 9:9)
20. Howl, O Heshbon, for ____ is spoiled. (Jer. 49:3)
21. He casteth forth his ____ like morsels. (Ps. 147:17)
22. When Merab Saul's daughter should have been given to David, that she was given unto ____. (1 Sam. 18:19)
26. Every ____, which my heavenly Father hath not planted, shall be rooted up. (Matt. 15:13)
29. Lod, and ____, the valley of craftsmen. (Neh. 11:35)
30. Scottish sailyard.
31. Of all which he hath given me I should ____ nothing. (John 6:39)
32. A man which ____ not on a wedding garment. (Matt. 22:11)
33. Caucasus native.
34. Of ____, the family of the Erites. (Num. 26:16)
35. ____, I perceive that thou art a prophet. (John 4:19)
36. ____ received their dead raised to life again. (Heb. 11:35)
37. And Poratha, and ____, and Aridatha. (Esther 9:8)
39. Having eyes full of adultery, and that cannot cease from ____. (2 Peter 2:14)
40. Guido's note.
41. To agree, and give their ____ unto the beast. (Rev. 17:17)
45. The children of ____ of Hezekiah, ninety and eight. (Neh. 7:21)
48. Charity, which is the ____ of perfectness. (Col. 3:14)
49. ____ hospitality one to another without grudging. (1 Peter 4:9)
50. This is ____, that we walk after his commandments. (2 John 6)
51. The Pharisees began to ____ him vehemently. (Luke 11:53)
52. We sailed to the ____ of Crete. (Acts 27:7 NIV)
53. Thou hast not ____ unto men, but unto God. (Acts 5:4)
54. A prophet mighty in ____ and word before God. (Luke 24:19)
55. Come. And ____ him that heareth say, Come. (Rev. 22:17)

Down

1. ____ for the day! for the day of the LORD. (Joel 1:15)
2. A ____ vision has been shown to me. (Isa. 21:2 NIV)
3. Our own souls, because ye were ____ unto us. (1 Thess. 2:8)
4. We gave you ____ orders not to teach. (Acts 5:28 NIV)
5. They gave him a ____ of a broiled fish. (Luke 24:42)
6. Mean while accusing or ____ excusing one another. (Rom. 2:15)
7. His body was ____ with the dew of heaven. (Dan. 4:33)
8. Flight of steps.
9. Jacob sojourned in the land of ____. (Ps. 105:23)
10. I have made you a tester of metals and my people the ____. (Jer. 6:27 NIV)
11. Blind, or broken, or maimed, or having a ____. (Lev. 22:22)
19. I am the ____, ye are the branches. (John 15:5)
20. Why make ye this ____, and weep? (Mark 5:39)
22. ____ immediately the ship was at the land. (John 6:21)

23. Duke Magdiel, duke ____: these be the dukes of Edom. (Gen. 36:43)
24. Tremble, ye women that are at ____. (Isa. 32:11)
25. Lay (obs. form).
26. Judgment, between blood and blood, between ____ and plea. (Deut. 17:8)
27. Ye ought to say, If the ____ will, we shall live. (James 4:15)
28. Because he would not spend the time in ____. (Acts 20:16)
29. All that handle the ____, the mariners. (Ezek. 27:29)
32. Parrot hawk.
33. How ____, O Lord, holy and true. (Rev. 6:10)
35. ____ thou here in a good place. (James 2:3)
36. Out of breath.

38. They will pursue us until we have ____ them away from the city. (Josh. 8:6 NIV)
39. Superficial burn.
41. ____ the son of Imnah the Levite. (2 Chron. 31:14)
42. Seeing ye are ____ of hearing. (Heb. 5:11)
43. As he saith also in ____, I will call them my people. (Rom. 9:25)
44. Sanctified, and ____ for the master's use. (2 Tim. 2:21)
45. The Spirit searcheth ____ things. (1 Cor. 2:10)
46. ____ sent Joram his son unto king David. (2 Sam. 8:10)
47. Adam called his wife's name ____. (Gen. 3:20)
48. It hath no stalk: the ____ shall yield no meal. (Hos. 8:7)

17

7

Across

1. Heber, which was the son of ____. (Luke 3:35)
5. They filled them up to the ____. (John 2:7)
9. There is a ____ here, which hath five barley loaves. (John 6:9)
12. He that biddeth him God speed is partaker of his ____ deeds. (2 John 11)
13. Sanballat sent his ____ to me. (Neh. 6:5 NIV)
14. Diminutive suffix.
15. I ____ with them, and cursed them. (Neh. 13:25)
17. Dutch liter.
18. Twixt's companion.
19. By the ____ of the countenance the heart is made better. (Eccles. 7:3)
21. The name of the wicked shall ____. (Prov. 10:7)
23. The commandment, deceived me, and by it ____ me. (Rom. 7:11)
24. Unclean for you: the weasel, the ____. (Lev. 11:29 NIV)
27. ____, when it is finished, bringeth forth death. (James 1:15)
29. ____ no more than that which is appointed you. (Luke 3:13)
32. An half ____ of land, which a yoke of oxen might plow. (1 Sam. 14:14)
34. Andrew his brother casting a ____ into the sea. (Mark 1:16)
36. He that sat upon him was called Faithful and ____. (Rev. 19:11)
37. Dan is a lion's ____: he shall leap from Bashan. (Deut. 33:22)
39. They also may without the word be ____ by the conversation of the wives. (1 Peter 3:1)
41. If I be lifted up from the earth, will draw all ____ unto me. (John 12:32)
42. It will be built again, with plaza and ____. (Dan. 9:25 NASB)
44. She drove the ____ through his temple. (Judg. 4:21 NIV)
46. Turning him to the body said, ____ arise. (Acts 9:40)

49. Smote him in Samaria, in the palace of the king's house, with Argob and ____. (2 Kings 15:25)
53. The same anointing teacheth you of ____ things. (1 John 2:27)
54. This mystery is great; but I am speaking with ____ to Christ and the church. (Eph. 5:32 NASB)
56. We passed to the ____ of a small island called Cauda. (Acts 27:16 NIV)
57. Algerian port.
58. Female nickname.
59. He saw no man: but they ____ him by the hand. (Acts 9:8)
60. As our ____ Jesus Christ hath shewed me. (2 Peter 1:14)
61. I looked, and, behold, a ____ was opened in heaven. (Rev. 4:1)

Down

1. After the most straitest ____ of our religion. (Acts 26:5)
2. To declare as fact.
3. Not to boast in another man's ____ of things. (2 Cor. 10:16)
4. My covenant will I not break, nor ____. (Ps. 89:34)
5. Achar, who brought disaster on Israel by violating the ____. (1 Chron. 2:7 NIV)
6. Eliminates.
7. You are bringing some strange ____. (Acts 17:20 NIV)
8. ____ not with him that flattereth with his lips. (Prov. 20:19)
9. Thou art ____, and neither cold nor hot. (Rev. 3:16)
10. ____ for all the evil abominations of the house! (Ezek. 6:11)
11. Filled his holes with prey, and his ____ with ravin. (Nah. 2:12)
16. ____, which was the son of Seth. (Luke 3:38)
20. The ____ sabbath day came almost the whole city. (Acts 13:44)
22. Purge away thy dross, and take away all thy ____. (Isa. 1:25)

Crossword Grid

1	2	3	4	■	5	6	7	8	■	9	10	11
12			■	13						14		
15			16						■	17		
18			■	19			20					
■		21	■	22	■	23					■	■
24	25	26	■	27		28	■	29			30	31
32			33		34		35		36			
37			38		39		40		■	41		
■		42		■	43	■	44		45		■	■
46	47				48		49			50	51	52
53			■	54			55				
56			■	57			■	58			
59			■	60			■	61			

24. Eat not of it ____, nor sodden at all. (Exod. 12:9)

25. Indian mulberry.

26. Then Moses ____, and durst not behold. (Acts 7:32)

28. These men are full of ____ wine. (Acts 2:13)

30. Stage reminder.

31. When the ____ heard it, they began to be much displeased with James and John. (Mark 10:41)

33. ____, lama sabachthani? (Mark 15:34)

35. The coat was without seam, woven from the ____. (John 19:23)

38. Those whom the LORD has sent to ____ the earth. (Zech. 1:10 NASB)

40. Let us draw ____ with a true heart. (Heb. 10:22)

43. Animal-like (comb. form).

45. In their ____ these teachers will exploit you with stories they have made up. (2 Peter 2:3 NIV)

46. I will cut down the ____ cedars thereof. (Isa. 37:24)

47. To the sheltered side.

48. Many women were there beholding ____ off. (Matt. 27:55)

50. Whoso looketh ____ the perfect law of liberty. (James 1:25)

51. Outer prefix.

52. The dead shall ____ the voice of the Son of God. (John 5:25)

55. They cast out their young children, to the ____ they might not live. (Acts 7:19)

8

Across

1. As of fire, and it ____ upon each of them. (Acts 2:3)
4. Diminutive suffix.
8. Commanded him to be kept in Herod's judgment ____. (Acts 23:35)
12. He planteth an ____, and the rain doth nourish it. (Isa. 44:14)
13. Sandy places.
14. You should have eaten the goat in the sanctuary ____. (Lev. 10:18 NIV)
15. Animal constellation.
16. But have ____ the hidden things of dishonesty. (2 Cor. 4:2)
18. The holy women also, who ____ in God. (1 Peter 3:5)
20. American state (abbrev.).
21. Exclamations of surprise.
22. He led the flock to the backside of the ____. (Exod. 3:1)
26. The prison ____ found we shut with all safety. (Acts 5:23)
29. The prophet ____, David's seer. (2 Sam 24:11)
30. Blessed are the dead which ____ in the Lord. (Rev. 14:13)
31. My couch shall ____ my complaint. (Job 7:13)
32. No ____ hath seen God at any time. (1 John 4:12)
33. Criminal intent. ____ rea (Latin).
34. ____ not one to another. (Col. 3:9)
35. Get up! Pick up your ____ and walk. (John 5:8 NIV)
36. For this reason God ____ them a powerful delusion. (2 Thess. 2:11 NIV)
37. Know how ye ought to ____ every man. (Col. 4:6)
39. Keros, the children of ____, the children of Padon. (Neh. 7:47)
40. Commercial.
41. Cleanse your hands, ye ____. (James 4:8)
45. Made a little lower than the angels for the ____ of death. (Heb. 2:9)
49. Naphtali is a ____ set free. (Gen. 49:21 NIV)
50. Saith also in ____, I will call them my people. (Rom. 9:25)
51. The Pharisees began to ____ him vehemently. (Luke 11:53)
52. The serpent beguiled ____ through his subtilty. (2 Cor. 11:3)
53. The hart, and the roebuck, and the fallow ____. (Deut. 14:5)
54. Jotham ran away, and fled, and went to ____. (Judg. 9:21)
55. Behold a great ____ dragon, having seven heads. (Rev. 12:3)

Down

1. Have ____ in yourselves, and have peace one with another. (Mark 9:50)
2. The daughter of Phanuel, of the tribe of ____. (Luke 2:36)
3. When ____ wast under the fig tree, I saw thee. (John 1:48)
4. The first man is of the earth, ____. (1 Cor. 15:47)
5. Now also the axe is laid unto the root of the ____. (Luke 3:9)
6. The diligent ____ only to plenteousness. (Prov. 21:5)
7. Self.
8. Lift up the ____ which hang down. (Heb. 12:12)
9. Rainbow's shape.
10. We . . . passed to the ____ of Cyprus. (Acts 27:4 NIV)
11. God hath heard the voice of the ____. (Gen. 21:17)
17. Neither at any time ____ we flattering words. (1 Thess. 2:5)
19. The dove found no rest for the ____ of her foot. (Gen. 8:9)
22. ____ shall be a serpent by the way. (Gen. 49:17)
23. This land that was desolate is become like the garden of ____. (Ezek. 36:35)
24. Fruit coat.
25. Hardy lady.
26. Web-like membrane.

27. Shut heaven, that it ____ not in the days of their prophecy. (Rev. 11:6)
28. Maintain good works for necessary ____. (Titus 3:14)
29. The pains of hell ____ hold upon me. (Ps. 116:3)
32. They ____ my path, they set forward my calamity. (Job 30:13)
33. For I ____ not that other men be eased, and ye burdened. (2 Cor. 8:13)
35. In the first year of Darius the ____. (Dan. 11:1)
36. Heman a ____, the son of Joel. (1 Chron. 6:33)
38. A cake of oiled bread, and one ____. (Lev. 8:26)
39. Superficial burn.

41. Father.
42. The sons of Mushi; Mahli, and ____, and Jeremoth, three. (1 Chron. 23:23)
43. Where David himself and his men were accustomed to ____. (1 Sam. 30:31 NKJV)
44. Being born again, not of corruptible ____. (1 Peter 1:23)
45. Other holy offerings ____ they in pots. (2 Chron. 35:13)
46. The law is good, if a man ____ it lawfully. (1 Tim. 1:8)
47. Taking with them the ____ for divination. (Num. 22:7 NIV)
48. ____ them in their hands and eat the kernels. (Luke 6:1 NIV)

9

Across

1. ____ the son of Shobal begat Jahath. (1 Chron. 4:2)
7. Duck walk.
13. Demonstrate.
14. Thomas ____, American inventor.
15. Blessed are they that ____ his commandments. (Rev. 22:14)
16. Scope of knowledge.
17. Whosoever is born of God doth not commit ____. (1 John 3:9)
18. Wasserman reaction (abbrev.).
19. Wapiti.
21. Scottish writer.
23. Keros, the children of ____, the children of Padon. (Neh. 7:47)
24. God cannot be tempted with ____. (James 1:13)
26. How long will it be ____ thou be quiet? (Jer. 47:6)
27. Charity suffereth ____, and is kind. (1 Cor. 13:4)
28. Go up, O Elam: besiege, O ____. (Isa. 21:2)
30. The priest shall ____ them, including the head. (Lev. 1:12 NIV)
32. Jacob was ____; he did not believe them. (Gen. 45:26 NIV)
34. He asked for a ____ table, and wrote, saying, His name is John. (Luke 1:63)
37. ____ hath forsaken me, having loved this present world. (2 Tim. 4:10)
41. If the firstborn son be ____ that was hated. (Deut. 21:15)
42. Make bare the ____, uncover the thigh. (Isa. 47:2)
44. His ____ shall be in their foreheads. (Rev. 22:4)
45. Yellow bugle.
46. Nikola ____, American inventor.
48. American weight.
49. Spanish article.
50. Jephunneh, and Pispah, and ____. (1 Chron. 7:38)
51. The heavens ____ the works of thine hands. (Heb. 1:10)
53. Who also declared unto ____ your love in the Spirit. (Col. 1:8)
54. Fraulein's name (plural).
56. Tranquil.
58. Angel.
59. Many bodies of the ____ which slept arose. (Matt. 27:52)

Down

1. To ____ them that were under the law. (Gal. 4:5)
2. Develop.
3. Set them to lie in ambush between Beth-el and ____. (Josh. 8:12)
4. Written not with ____, but with the Spirit. (2 Cor. 3:3)
5. Holes in one.
6. Sir, if thou have borne him ____, tell me where. (John 20:15)
7. For the ____ border, ye shall even have the great sea. (Num. 34:6)
8. Passageway.
9. He will silence her noisy ____. (Jer. 51:55 NIV)
10. Dal segno [Italian, 'after the sign'] (abbrev.).
11. The ____ of the oxen which I hear. (1 Sam. 15:14)
12. Infuriate.
20. Thou never gavest me a ____, that I might make merry with my friends. (Luke 15:29)
22. Fruits.
23. I will be his God, and he shall be my ____. (Rev. 21:7)
25. Avoid stupid arguments, long ____ of ancestors. (Titus 3:9 GNB)
27. Come unto me, all ye that labour and are heavy ____. (Matt. 11:28)
29. Panay native.
31. The shield of his mighty men is made ____. (Nah. 2:3)
33. In my wrath I will ____ a violent wind. (Ezek. 13:13 NIV)

34. Agree with thine adversary quickly, ____ thou art in the way. (Matt. 5:25)

35. Show respect for the elderly and ____ your God. (Lev. 19:32 NIV)

36. ____ the son of Ikkesh the Tekoite. (1 Chron. 27:9)

38. The law forbids you to carry your ____. (John 5:10 NIV)

39. I will pay back four times the ____. (Luke 19:8 NIV)

40. Those who by reason of use have their ____ exercised to discern both good and evil. (Heb. 5:14)

43. Now we see through a ____ , darkly. (1 Cor. 13:12)

46. Let their table be made a snare, and a ____. (Rom. 11:9)

47. He has brought Greeks into the temple ____. (Acts 21:28 NIV)

50. Pseudonym acronym.

52. Of ____, the family of the Erites. (Num. 26:16)

55. Shuppim also, and Huppim, the children of ____. (1 Chron. 7:12)

57. There is a woman that hath a familiar spirit at ____-dor. (1 Sam. 28:7)

10

Across

1. He led captivity captive, ____ gave gifts unto men. (Eph. 4:8)
4. Thou ____ altogether born in sins. (John 9:34)
8. Tunisian measure.
12. Be thou cast into the ____; it shall be done. (Matt. 21:21)
13. Their ____ of pleasure is to carouse. (2 Peter 2:13 NIV)
14. Not only ____, but tattlers also and busy-bodies. (1 Tim. 5:13)
15. Gentle touch.
16. A leader and ____ to the people. (Isa. 55:4)
18. Meat slab.
20. Whatever was written in ____ times was written for our instruction. (Rom. 15:4 NASB)
21. Jesus the mediator of the ____ covenant. (Heb. 12:24)
23. Sheepfold.
24. Roboam begat Abia; and Abia begat ____. (Matt. 1:7)
27. The glory of God ____ lighten it. (Rev. 21:23)
29. Wherefore laying ____ all malice, and all guile. (1 Peter 2:1)
33. ____ obeyed Abraham, calling him lord. (1 Peter 3:6)
35. The Valley of Siddim was full of ____ pits. (Gen. 14:10 NIV)
37. Cretians are alway liars, evil beasts, ____ bellies (Titus 1:12)
38. The night is far ____, the day is at hand. (Rom. 13:12)
40. ____ once more I shake not the earth only. (Heb. 12:26)
42. We sailed to the ____ of Crete. (Acts 27:7 NIV)
43. Uzzi, and Uzziel, and Jerimoth, and ____. (1 Chron. 7:7)
45. The heaven over you is stayed from ____. (Hag. 1:10)
47. An ____ harder than flint have I made. (Ezek. 3:9)
51. Blessed is the one who ____ the words. (Rev. 1:3 NIV)

55. The heavens will ____ with a roar. (2 Peter 3:10 NIV)
57. ____ is a lion's whelp. (Deut. 33:22)
58. Seed coat.
59. Being knit together in love, and ____ all riches. (Col. 2:2)
60. Orinoco tributary.
61. Some ____ sins are open beforehand. (1 Tim. 5:24)
62. Caesar (Russian).
63. ____ the tree down, and destroy it. (Dan. 4:23)

Down

1. The poison of ____ is under their lips. (Rom. 3:13)
2. Orderly.
3. Give notice of the ____ when the days of purification would end. (Acts 21:26 NIV)
4. And that ____ one toucheth him not. (1 John 5:18)
5. Why make ye this ____, and weep? (Mark 5:39)
6. Flowery.
7. The son of David had a fair sister, whose name was ____. (2 Sam. 13:1)
8. Flawless.
9. Melchi, which was the son of ____. (Luke 3:28)
10. To the sheltered side.
11. German sir.
17. The children shouting in the temple ____. (Matt. 21:15 NIV)
19. He that is ____ hireling, and not the shepherd. (John 10:12)
22. We do you to ____ of the grace of God. (2 Cor. 8:1)
24. Cometh unto thee, meek, and sitting upon an ____. (Matt. 21:5)
25. The trees of the LORD are full of ____. (Ps. 104:16)
26. And ____ not his sisters here with us? (Mark 6:3)
28. And a thousand years as one ____ (2 Peter 3:8)

24

30. Love worketh no ____ to his neighbour. (Rom. 13:10)

31. Do you watch when the ____ bears her fawn? (Job 39:1 NIV)

32. What mean these seven ____ lambs? (Gen. 21:29)

34. He was with the wild ____, and angels attended him. (Mark 1:13 NIV)

36. Sing ye unto her, A vineyard of ____ wine. (Isa. 27:2)

39. For their welfare, let it become a ____. (Ps. 69:22)

41. Knowing therefore the ____ of the Lord, we persuade men. (2 Cor. 5:11)

44. Data entry.

46. Our liberty which ____ have in Christ Jesus. (Gal. 2:4)

47. Enoch also, the seventh from ____. (Jude 14)

48. A ____ vision has been shown to me. (Isa. 21:2 NIV)

49. Hindu month.

50. Rulers of hundreds, rulers of fifties, and rulers of ____. (Exod. 18:25)

52. ____ the daughter of Elon the Hittite. (Gen. 36:2)

53. None is so fierce that ____ stir him up. (Job 41:10)

54. Her Nazarites were purer than ____. (Lam. 4:7)

56. Zoological suffix.

11

Across

1. The ____ flesh is unclean: it is a leprosy. (Lev. 13:15)
4. ____ me your faith without deeds. (James 2:18 NIV)
8. The iron be blunt, and he do not whet the ____. (Eccles. 10:10)
12. Geber the son of ____ was in the country. (1 Kings 4:19)
13. Ungodly deeds which they ____ ungodly committed. (Jude 15)
14. That we may ____ a quiet and peaceable life. (1 Tim. 2:2)
15. Ye shall have tribulation ____ days. (Rev. 2:10)
16. The churches of ____ salute you. (1 Cor. 16:19)
17. A ship of Alexandria, which had wintered in the ____. (Acts 28:11)
18. ____ bare Abram a son. (Gen. 16:15)
20. O ye ____ bones, hear the word of the LORD. (Ezek. 37:4)
22. My tongue is the ____ of a ready writer. (Ps. 45:1)
23. That they might only touch the ____ of his garment. (Matt.14:36)
25. Partial (comb. form).
27. Pray (prefix).
30. Our brother Timothy is ____ at liberty. (Heb.13:23)
32. Touch not; ____ not; handle not. (Col. 2:21)
35. Let us not be weary in ____ doing. (Gal. 6:9)
37. Upon the great ____ of their right foot. (Exod. 29:20)
39. A Prophet was beforetime called a ____. (1 Sam. 9:9)
40. My fellowlabourers, whose ____ are in the book of life. (Phil. 4:3)
42. Anger.
44. ____ that ye love one another with a pure heart. (1 Peter 1:22)
45. We know that an ____ is nothing in the world. (1 Cor. 8:4)
47. The breath of God produces ____. (Job 37:10 NIV)
49. He was a thief, and had the ____. (John 12:6)
51. Doth not your master ____ tribute? (Matt. 17:24)
53. The seed of an ____ shall yield an ephah. (Isa. 5:10)
57. Even in laughter the heart may ____. (Prov. 14:13 NIV)
59. Brazilian woman of rank.
61. Adam called his wife's name ____. (Gen. 3:20)
62. Many of them also which used curious ____ brought their books together, and burned them. (Acts 19:19)
63. Of Jerahmeel were, Maaz, and Jamin, and ____. (1 Chron. 2:27)
64. But ye have made it a ____ of thieves. (Luke 19:46)
65. Bets.
66. Find grace to help in time of ____. (Heb. 4:16)
67. The ____ of the commandment is charity. (1 Tim. 1:5)

Down

1. Boaz begat Obed of ____. (Matt. 1:5)
2. He spoke these words while teaching in the temple ____. (John 8:20 NIV)
3. Under it shall dwell all fowl of every ____. (Ezek. 17:23)
4. He who ____ my bread has lifted up his heel against me. (John 13:18 NIV)
5. Lord ____ commanded that those who preach the gospel should receive their living from the gospel. (1 Cor. 9:14 NIV)
6. Roman poet.
7. My zeal ____ me out. (Ps. 119:139 NIV)
8. ____ thought she had been drunken. (1 Sam. 1:13)
9. He who ignores discipline ____ himself. (Prov. 15:32 NIV)
10. The wind, like chaff swept away by a ____. (Job 21:18 NIV)
11. The land of Nod, on the east of ____. (Gen. 4:16)
19. ____, thou that destroyest the temple. (Mark 15:29)
21. Now we see not ____ all things put under him. (Heb. 2:8)
24. But was in that place where Martha ____ him. (John 11:30)

26. Male plant.
27. He is drawn away of his ____ lust, and enticed. (James 1:14)
28. Tumeric.
29. He treadeth the winepress of the fierceness and wrath of ____ God. (Rev. 19:15)
31. ____ sent Joram his son unto king David. (2 Sam. 8:10)
33. Where the drive begins.
34. How long will it be ____ they believe? (Num. 14:11)
36. If ye be ____ of the Spirit, ye are not under the law. (Gal. 5:18)
38. Of ____, the family of the Erites. (Num. 26:16)
41. He it is, to whom I shall give a ____. (John 13:26)
43. Plant water.

46. Ah sinful nation, a people ____ with iniquity. (Isa. 1:4)
48. Daybreak (comb. form).
49. Seven thousand men, who have not bowed the knee to the image of ____. (Rom. 11:4)
50. An half ____ of land, which a yoke of oxen might plow. (1 Sam. 14:14)
52. My ____ is easy, and my burden is light. (Matt. 11:30)
54. In the first year of Darius the ____. (Dan. 11:1)
55. Reward her ____ as she rewarded you. (Rev. 18:6)
56. Let us not ____ it, but cast lots for it. (John 19:24)
58. Tee's predecessor.
60. Used to identify woman's maiden name.

12

Across

1. Sin, taking occasion by the commandment, deceived me, and by it ____ me. (Rom. 7:11)
5. ____ times of refreshing shall come from the presence of the Lord. (Acts 3:19)
8. Greek portal.
12. Tyndareus' wife.
13. Aaron . . . when he died in mount ____. (Num. 33:39)
14. Let it alone this ____ also, till I shall dig. (Luke 13:8)
15. They ____ him by the blood of the Lamb. (Rev. 12:11)
17. It is a ____ thing that the king requireth. (Dan. 2:11)
18. Do count them but dung, that I may ____ Christ. (Phil. 3:8)
19. Every ____ that loveth is born of God. (1 John 4:7)
20. And they fled before the men of ____. (Josh. 7:4)
21. Let him ____ in faith, nothing wavering. (James 1:6)
22. Paul stood on the ____ and beckoned with the hand. (Acts 21:40)
26. The night is far ____, the day is at hand. (Rom. 13:12)
29. If any man will ____ thee at the law. (Matt. 5:40)
30. We put out to sea again and passed to the ____ of Cyprus. (Acts 27:4 NIV)
31. The ____ also calved in the field, and forsook it. (Jer. 14:5)
32. The ____ of truth shall be established for ever. (Prov. 12:19)
33. The earth which drinketh in the ____. (Heb. 6:7)
34. Lod, and ____, the valley of craftsmen. (Neh. 11:35)
35. The birds of the ____ have nests. (Luke 9:58)
36. Aaron the ____ of the LORD. (Ps. 106:16)
37. The way that goeth down from Jerusalem unto Gaza, which is ____. (Acts 8:26)
39. We ____ our bread with the peril of our lives. (Lam. 5:9)
40. Judgment must begin ____ the house of God. (1 Peter 4:17)
41. Ye do ____, not knowing the scriptures. (Matt. 22:29)
42. Thou ____ the corners of thy beard. (Lev. 19:27)
45. Standing ____ off for the fear of her torment. (Rev. 18:10)
48. Every ____ of God is good and nothing is refused. (1 Tim. 4:4)
50. Show me the ____ used for paying the tax. (Matt. 22:19 NIV)
51. Two are better than ____. (Eccles. 4:9)
52. He saith also in ____, I will call them my people. (Rom. 9:25)
53. And he said I will not destroy it for ____ sake. (Gen. 18:32)
54. They are ____ with the showers of the mountains. (Job 24:8)
55. Italicized (abbrev.).

Down

1. O fools, and ____ of heart to believe. (Luke 24:25)
2. He saw ____ the son of Alphaeus. (Mark 2:14)
3. The land is as the garden of ____ before them. (Joel 2:3)
4. In righteousness he doth judge and make ____. (Rev. 19:11)
5. I ____ God, whom I serve from my forefathers. (2 Tim. 1:3)
6. Learn first to shew piety at ____. (1 Tim. 5:4)
7. How long will it be ____ they attain to innocency? (Hos. 8:5)
8. When Cyrenius was governor of ____. (Luke 2:2)
9. Caffeinic beverage.
10. All that handle the ____, the mariners. (Ezek. 27:29)
11. There ____ yet four months, and then cometh harvest. (John 4:35)
16. Neither will I offer burnt offerings unto the LORD my God of that which doth ____ me nothing. (2 Sam. 24:24)
20. I ____ no pleasant bread. (Dan. 10:3)
21. Say in a word, ____ my servant shall be healed. (Luke 7:7)
22. I will come in to him, and will ____ with him. (Rev. 3:20)
23. Hushathite, ____ the Ahohite. (1 Chron. 11:29)

24. I will give free ____ to my complaint. (Job 10:1 NIV)
25. Preached the gospel unto you with the Holy Ghost ____ down from heaven. (1 Peter 1:12)
26. Be ____ with sandals; and not put on two coats. (Mark 6:9)
27. Our sins be upon us, and we ____ away in them. (Ezek. 33:10)
28. ____, which was the son of Seth. (Luke 3:38)
29. ____, we would see Jesus. (John 12:21)
32. Your lightning ____ up the world. (Ps 77:18 NIV)
33. Unclean for you: the weasel, the ____, any kind of great lizard, the gecko. (Lev. 11:29 NIV)
35. Thou ____ worthy to take the book. (Rev. 5:9)
36. ____ herself received strength to conceive. (Heb. 11:11)

38. The wicked man ____ deceptive wages. (Prov. 11:18 NIV)
39. ____ Priscilla and Aquila (Rom. 16:3)
41. Sea eagle.
42. A bishop ____ be blameless, as the steward of God. (Titus 1:7)
43. To a remote ____ in the hill country of Ephraim where I live. (Judg. 19:18 NIV)
44. The earth shall ____ to and fro like a drunkard. (Isa. 24:20)
45. This woman was taken in adultery, in the very ____. (John 8:4)
46. The wicked ____ pulls all of them up with hooks. (Hab. 1:15 NIV)
47. Riblah, on the east side of ____. (Num. 34:11)
48. The ____ and the bear shall feed. (Isa. 11:7)
49. Hadadezer had wars with ____. (2 Sam. 8:10)

13

Across

1. "Down with" (French).
5. To his sin he ____ rebellion. (Job 34:37 NIV)
9. One ____ or one tittle shall in no wise pass. (Matt. 5:18)
12. The ____ shall understand knowledge. (Isa. 32:4)
13. The stream ____ vehemently upon that house. (Luke 6:48)
14. Fuegan Indian.
15. Scottish broth.
16. ____ Lot's wife. (Luke 17:32)
18. After these things, that God did tempt ____. (Gen. 22:1)
20. The king of ____ they took alive, and brought him to Joshua. (Josh. 8:23)
21. And ____ begat Amminadab. (Ruth 4:19)
22. An arrogant person never ____ he is wrong. (Prov. 13:1 GNB)
26. She painted her face, and ____ her head. (2 Kings 9:30)
29. To ____ them that dwell upon the earth. (Rev. 3:10)
30. The gods.
31. King ____ the Canaanite, which dwelt in the south. (Num. 33:40)
32. ____ king of Hamath heard that David had smitten all the host of Hadadezer. (2 Sam. 8:9)
33. Covet earnestly the ____ gifts. (1 Cor. 12:31)
34. Mythic bird.
35. The ____ shall take him by the heel. (Job 18:9)
36. Blackboard material.
37. ____ your servants to speak your word. (Acts 4:29 NIV)
39. Small (Scottish).
40. Two (Roman).
41. A name written, that no man knew, but he ____. (Rev.19:12)
45. Cooking surfaces.
49. ____ answered and said, Am not I a Benjamite, of the smallest of the tribes? (1 Sam. 9:21)

50. And ____ with her suburbs, and Juttah with her suburbs. (Josh. 21:16)
51. Ireland.
52. Jacob have I loved, but ____ have I hated. (Rom. 9:13)
53. Were there not ____ cleansed? but where are the nine? (Luke 17:17)
54. The hart, and the roebuck, and the fallow ____. (Deut 14:5)
55. Between un and trois.

Down

1. ____ was a great man among the Anakims. (Josh. 14:15)
2. Point.
3. Anna, a prophetess, the daughter of Phanuel, of the tribe of ____. (Luke 2:36)
4. The peg driven into the firm place will give way; it will be ____ off. (Isa. 22:25 NIV)
5. Hagar bare Ishmael to ____. (Gen. 16:16)
6. Those members of the body, which we ____ less honorable. (1 Cor. 12:23 NASB)
7. Thou shalt in any wise let the ____ go. (Deut. 22:7)
8. His hands were ____ until the going down of the sun. (Exod. 17:12)
9. There was a man in the land of Uz, whose name was ____. (Job. 1:1)
10. Ye have an unction from the Holy ____. (1 John 2:20)
11. They used brick instead of stone, and ____ instead of mortar. (Gen. 11:3 NIV)
17. Arabic letter.
19. It ____ been better for them not to have known the way. (2 Peter 2:21)
22. Biblical lion.
23. "Is that your own ____," Jesus asked. (John 18:34 NIV)
24. ____ everything. Hold on to the good. (1 Thess. 5:21 NIV)
25. Rebuild this house of God on its ____. (Ezra 6:7 NIV)
26. The devil threw him down, and ____ him. (Luke 9:42)

27. They came unto the ____ gate that leadeth unto the city. (Acts 12:10)

28. Whosoever shall say to his brother, ____, shall be in danger of the council. (Matt. 5:22)

29. Long or short weight.

32. ____ the kine to the cart, and bring their calves. (1 Sam. 6:7)

33. ____ is the man that endureth temptation. (James 1:12)

35. A spirit ____ past my face. (Job 4:15 NIV)

36. Arphaxad, which was the son of ____. (Luke 3:36)

38. Receive him not into your house, neither ____ him God speed. (2 John 10)

39. The foolishness of God is ____ than men. (1 Cor. 1:25)

41. And ____ is the mind which hath wisdom. (Rev. 17:9)

42. Take thine ____, eat, drink, and be merry. (Luke 12:19)

43. Hawaiian feast.

44. Publius lay sick of a fever and of a bloody ____. (Acts 28:8)

45. Abraham ____ up early in the morning. (Gen. 19:27)

46. But the wheat and the ____ were not smitten. (Exod. 9:32)

47. Brought him to an ____, and took care of him. (Luke 10:34)

48. ____ not one to another, seeing that ye have put off the old man. (Col. 3:9)

14

Across

1. Lo, in her mouth was an olive ____. (Gen. 8:11)
5. The dumb ____ speaking with man's voice forbade the madness of the prophet. (2 Peter 2:16)
8. Say ye unto your brethren, ____. (Hos. 2:1)
12. Also Bakbukiah and ____, their brethren. (Neh. 12:9)
13. ____ sent Joram his son unto king David. (2 Sam. 8:10)
14. For the ____ is not dead, but sleepeth. (Matt. 9:24)
15. There is a bad ____, for he has been there four days. (John 11:39 NIV)
16. I am like an ____ of the desert. (Ps. 102:6)
17. Shield rim.
18. Dutch liter.
20. Profited in the Jews' religion above many my ____. (Gal. 1:14)
22. You have lifted up the ____ of Moloch. (Acts 7:43 NIV)
25. Moses called Oshea the son of ____. (Num. 13:16)
26. Yet offend in one ____, he is guilty of all. (James 2:10)
27. They came out as a whirlwind to ____ me. (Hab. 3:14)
31. Bolivian Indian.
32. ____ that ye love one another with a pure heart. (1 Peter 1:22)
33. Adam was first formed, then ____. (1 Tim. 2:13)
34. Bondage, and ____ them evil four hundred years. (Acts 7:6)
37. Bethany was less than two ____ from Jerusalem. (John 11:18 NIV)
39. ____ yourselves likewise with the same mind. (1 Peter 4:1)
40. This is a ____ place, and the time is now past. (Matt. 14:15)
41. This Agar is mount Sinai in ____. (Gal. 4:25)
44. They do alway ____ in their heart. (Heb. 3:10)
45. Backward pointing snag.

46. He ____ before, and climbed up into a sycamore tree. (Luke 19:4)
48. Death reigned from ____ to Moses. (Rom. 5:14)
52. Madder shrub genus.
53. Uzzi, and Uzziel, and Jerimoth, and ____. (1 Chron. 7:7)
54. Woe to them that are at ____ in Zion. (Amos 6:1)
55. ____ was tender eyed; but Rachel was beautiful. (Gen. 29:17)
56. ____ for perfection, listen to my appeal. (2 Cor. 13:11 NIV)
57. Easy gait.

Down

1. Nilotic negro.
2. Overcometh, and keepeth my works unto the ____. (Rev. 2:26)
3. Upward (comb. form).
4. Greek measure equal to one bath.
5. To put an end to sin, to ____ for wickedness. (Dan. 9:24 NIV)
6. Sir, didst not thou ____ good seed in thy field (Matt. 13:27)
7. Put to ____ the ignorance of foolish men. (1 Peter 2:15)
8. I will pay back four times the ____. (Luke 19:8 NIV)
9. Call me not Naomi, call me ____. (Ruth 1:20)
10. Two women shall be grinding at the ____. (Matt. 24:41)
11. March fifteenth.
19. Go to the ____, thou sluggard; consider her ways. (Prov. 6:6)
21. Sine ____ non.
22. Drink ye, and be drunken, and ____, and fall. (Jer. 25:27)
23. Hath raised up an ____ of salvation for us. (Luke 1:69)
24. That count it pleasure to ____ in the day time. (2 Peter 2:13)
27. It is ____ on fire of hell. (James 3:6)

1	2	3	4	█	5	6	7	█	8	9	10	11
12				█	13			█	14			
15				█	16			█	17			
█	█	█	18	19		█	20	21				
22	23	24				█	25			█	█	█
26					█	27				28	29	30
31			█	█	32			█	33			
34		█	35	36		█	37	38				
█	█	█	39			█	40					
41	42	43				█	44			█	█	█
45				█	46	47		█	48	49	50	51
52				█	53			█	54			
55				█	56			█	57			

28. Prefix meaning distant.
29. Which dwelleth in us, and shall be with us for ____. (2 John 2)
30. That they should ____ yet for a little season. (Rev. 6:11)
32. There cometh a woman of ____ to draw water. (John 4:7)
35. I will make ____ a stable for camels. (Ezek. 25:5)
36. Of ____, the family of the Erites. (Num. 26:16)
37. Sea (French).
38. Rabbi, thou art the Son of God; thou art the King of ____. (John 1:49)

40. Levi material.
41. From the blood of righteous ____ unto the blood of Zacharias. (Matt. 23:35)
42. Verbally irrational.
43. He made a whip out of cords, and drove all from the temple ____. (John 2:15 NIV)
47. Biblical lion.
49. Philippine tree.
50. The suckling child shall play on the hole of the ____. (Isa. 11:8)
51. Indian tree.

15

Across

1. That Tyrus hath said against Jerusalem, ____. (Ezek. 26:2)
4. The heavens shall ____ away with a great noise. (2 Peter 3:10)
8. Mattathias, which was the son of ____. (Luke 3:25)
12. Gibbon, spirit.
13. It vomited Jonah up ____ the dry land. (Jonah 2:10 NASB)
14. ____ it, even to the foundation. (Ps. 137:7)
15. Jephunneh, and Pispah, and ____. (1 Chron. 7:38)
16. Quick, let me have some of that red ____! (Gen. 25:30 NIV)
17. Say unto this sycamine ____, Be thou plucked up. (Luke 17:6)
18. The eleventh month, which is the month ____. (Zech. 1:7)
20. The ____ of the scribes is in vain. (Jer. 8:8)
22. ____, which was the son of Noe. (Luke 3:36)
23. Behold, I make all things ____. (Rev. 21:5)
25. Can the ____ grow up without mire? (Job 8:11)
27. Shall I come unto you with a ____, or in love? (1 Cor. 4:21)
30. It shall be seven days under the ____. (Lev. 22:27)
32. I ____ God, whom I serve from my fore-fathers. (1 Tim. 1:3)
35. The sons of Ulla; ____, and Haniel, and Rezia. (1 Chron. 7:39)
37. ____ peradventure for a good man some would even dare to die. (Rom. 5:7)
39. ____, lama sabachthani? (Mark 15:34)
40. You are from ____, I am from above. (John 8:23 NASB)
42. Thou art neither cold ____ hot. (Rev. 3:15)
44. He was ____ as a sheep to the slaughter. (Acts 8:32)
45. Made us ____ to be partakers of the inheri-tance. (Col. 1:12)
47. Cast the ____ on the right side of the ship. (John 21:6)
49. Maachah the mother of ____ the king. (2 Chron. 15:16)
51. The sons of Bela; Ezbon, and Uzzi, and Uzziel, and Jerimoth, and ____, five. (1 Chron. 7:7)
53. ____, if you hear his voice, do not harden your hearts. (Heb. 4:7 NIV)
57. Write it before them in a table, and ____ it in a book. (Isa. 30:8)
59. The churches of ____ salute you. (1 Cor. 16:19)
61. Who ____ kept by the power of God through faith. (1 Peter 1:5)
62. Girl's name.
63. Sibbecai the Hushathite, ____ the Ahohite. (1 Chron. 11:29)
64. We sailed over the ____ of Cilicia. (Acts 27:5)
65. Our epistle written in our hearts, known and ____ of all men. (2 Cor. 3:2)
66. Confederate state (abbrev.).
67. Fog (Scottish).

Down

1. ____ for the day! (Joel 1:15)
2. And the ____, and the coney. (Deut. 14:7)
3. ____, and Dumah, and Eshean. (Josh. 15:52)
4. I have ____ watchmen on your walls. (Isa. 62:6 NIV)
5. Go to the ____, thou sluggard. (Prov. 6:6)
6. There is but a ____ between me and death. (1 Sam. 20:3)
7. The ____ soweth the word. (Mark 4:14)
8. Thou ____ my Son, to day have I begotten thee. (Heb. 5:5)
9. Peter ____, Senate chaplain and author.
10. As he saith also in ____, I will call them my people, which were not my people. (Rom. 9:25)
11. If any man ____ to be contentious, we have no such custom. (1 Cor. 11:16)
19. No man put a stumblingblock or ____ occa-sion to fall. (Rom. 14:13)
21. I went down to the grove of ____ trees. (Song of Songs 6:11 NIV)
24. The ____ of truth shall be evil spoken of. (2 Peter 2:2)
26. The wife see that ____ reverence her hus-band. (Eph. 5:33)

27. God will hear all the words of ____-shakeh. (2 Kings 19:4)

28. Copper is smelted from ____. (Job 28:2 NIV)

29. Crescens to Galatia, Titus unto ____. (2 Tim. 4:10)

31. The tabernacle of God is with ____. (Rev. 21:3)

33. As it was in the days of ____, so shall it be. (Luke 17:26)

34. Thou never gavest me a ____, that I might make merry with my friends. (Luke 15:29)

36. For all the hills once cultivated by the ____. (Isa. 7:25 NIV)

38. American weight

41. Chinese dynasty.

43. They did not like to ____ God in their knowledge (Rom. 1:28)

46. Feature.

48. ____ him be glory and dominion for ever and ever. (Rev. 1:6)

49. Esh-col, and brother of ____: and these were confederate with Abram. (Gen. 14:13)

50. James and John, and began to be ____ amazed. (Mark 14:33)

52. They had gone through the ____ unto Paphos. (Acts 13:6)

54. Lest at any time thou ____ thy foot against a stone. (Matt. 4:6)

55. The children shouting in the temple ____. (Matt. 21:15 NIV)

56. Continue there a ____, and buy and sell. (James 4:13)

58. Having neither beginning of days, nor ____ of life. (Heb. 7:3)

60. John (Gaelic).

16

Across

1. The ____ and warrior, the judge and prophet. (Isa. 3:2 NIV)
5. Pierce his ear with an ____. (Exod. 21:6 NIV)
8. ____ ye away, thou inhabitant of Saphir. (Micah 1:11)
12. The blessing upon mount Gerizim, and the curse upon mount ____. (Deut. 11:29)
13. And [Peter] did cast himself into the ____. (John 21:7)
14. Terror, consumption, and the burning ____, that shall consume the eyes, and cause sorrow. (Lev. 26:16)
15. The glory of the LORD shall be thy ____. (Isa. 58:8)
17. Claudius had commanded all Jews to depart from ____. (Acts 18:2)
18. How long will it be ____ they attain to innocency? (Hos. 8:5)
19. Given to hospitality, ____ to teach. (1 Tim. 3:2)
20. Howl, O Heshbon, for ____ is spoiled. (Jer. 49:3)
21. He planteth an ____, and the rain doth nourish it. (Isa. 44:14)
22. And shall ____ our hearts before him. (1 John 3:19)
26. To ____ under his feet all the prisoners. (Lam. 3:34)
29. I wrote them with ____ in the book. (Jer. 36:18)
30. Be not, as the hypocrites, of a ____ countenance. (Matt. 6:16)
31. What ____ you that you keep on arguing? (Job 16:3 NIV)
32. ____ the son of Ikkesh the Tekoite. (1 Chron. 27:9)
33. For thy ransom, Ethiopia and ____ for thee. (Isa. 43:3)
34. And were all baptized unto Moses in the cloud and in the ____. (1 Cor. 10:2)
35. Pressure abbreviation.
36. Baal-hanan the son of Achbor died, and ____ reigned in his stead. (Gen. 36:39)
37. I will send you ____ the prophet. (Mal. 4:5)
39. After the ____ Satan entered into him. (John 13:27)
40. A woman that hath a familiar spirit at ____-dor. (1 Sam. 28:7)
41. Go ahead and take your ____. (Prov. 24:33 GNB)
42. ____ the son of Abdiel, the son of Guni. (1 Chron. 5:15)
45. Put them under ____, and under harrows of iron. (2 Sam. 12:31)
48. Greatly offended, and ____ himself upon them. (Ezek. 25:12)
50. By faith Isaac blessed Jacob and ____. (Heb. 11:20)
51. Look on the fields; for they ____ white already. (John 4:35)
52. They shall ____ as lions' whelps. (Jer. 51:38)
53. Pitches.
54. The land of ____, on the east of Eden. (Gen. 4:16)
55. Hawaiian chant.

Down

1. Behold, a greater than Jonas is ____. (Matt. 12:41)
2. Shem also the father of all the children of ____ (Gen. 10:21)
3. It is a ____ thing that the king requireth. (Dan. 2:11)
4. Oil suffix.
5. Joah, the son of ____, the recorder. (Isa. 36:22)
6. I would thou ____ cold or hot. (Rev. 3:15)
7. There is a ____ here, which hath five barley loaves. (John 6:9)
8. French capital.
9. I knew a man in Christ above fourteen years ____. (2 Cor. 12:2)
10. With a great ____ obtained I this freedom. (Acts 22:28)
11. The man of wisdom shall ____ thy name. (Micah 6:9)
16. Be baptized, and ____ away thy sins. (Acts 22:16)
20. Whatsoever we ____, we receive. (1 John 3:22)
21. A wild ____ used to the wilderness. (Jer. 2:24)
22. Literary scraps.
23. Neither at any time ____ we flattering words. (1 Thess. 2:5)
24. Danube tributary.

25. Israel journeyed, and spread his tent beyond the tower of ____. (Gen. 35:21)
26. Ye shall in no ____ enter into the kingdom. (Matt. 5:20)
27. Red River rebel.
28. I heard a man's voice between the banks of ____. (Dan. 8:16)
29. Ezbon, and Uzzi, and Uzziel, and Jerimoth, and ____, five. (1 Chron. 7:7)
32. ____-bosheth the son of Saul. (2 Sam. 2:8)
33. The trees of the LORD are full of ____. (Ps. 104:16)
35. Thy oblation be a meat offering baken in a ____. (Lev. 2:5)
36. Looking for that blessed ____. (Titus 2:13)
38. ____, who was made a little lower than the angels. (Heb. 2:9)

39. He ____ others; let him save himself. (Luke 23:35)
41. Paul was brought before ____. (2 Tim. subscr.)
42. Shammah the son of ____. (2 Sam. 23:11)
43. His name that sat on him was Death, and ____. (Rev. 6:8)
44. Their words seemed to them as ____ tales. (Luke 24:11)
45. He hath ____ the world in their heart. (Eccles. 3:11)
46. Hanani the seer came to ____. (2 Chron. 16:7)
47. He teacheth my hands to ____. (Ps. 18:34)
48. As the lad ____, he shot an arrow. (1 Sam. 20:36)
49. Falstaff's follower.

17

Across

1. Maimed, or having a ____ , or scurvy, or scabbed. (Lev. 22:22)
4. An habitation of dragons, and a court for ____. (Isa. 34:13)
8. Let him ____ your left cheek too. (Matt. 5:39 GNB)
12. Common suffix.
13. There was a continual ____ given him of the king. (Jer. 52:34)
14. The ____ and warrior, the judge and prophet. (Isa. 3:2 NIV)
15. ____, give me this water, that I thirst not. (John 4:15)
16. Glacial ridge.
17. Seth lived after he begat ____. (Gen. 5:7)
18. ____ had waited till Job had spoken. (Job 32:4)
20. Jacob sojourned in the land of ____. (Ps. 105:23)
22. Take the girdle that thou hast ____. (Jer. 13:4)
23. Do ye not therefore ____; because ye know not the scriptures, neither the power of God? (Mark 12:24)
25. A wild olive tree, ____ graffed in among them. (Rom. 11:17)
27. Brazilian tree.
30. Let no man ____ when he is tempted, I am tempted of God. (James 1:13)
32. The sons of his wife Hodiah the sister of ____. (1 Chron. 4:19)
35. Yea, many shall make ____ unto thee. (Job 11:19)
37. French pronoun.
39. When Paul was brought before ____. (2 Tim. subscr.)
40. That which I do I ____ not. (Rom. 7:15)
42. The Valley of Siddim was full of ____ pits. (Gen. 14:10 NIV)
44. This is my blood of the ____ testament. (Matt. 26:28)
45. Came back with Naomi out of the country of ____. (Ruth 2:6)
47. The heavens shall give their ____. (Zech. 8:12)
49. As it was in the days of ____, so shall it be. (Luke 17:26)

51. I will ____ evil beasts out of the land. (Lev. 26:6)
53. She bare him Zimran, and Jokshan, and ____. (Gen. 25:2)
57. ____, a prophetess, the daughter of Phanuel. (Luke 2:36)
59. Behold, a ____ is in thine own eye? (Matt. 7:4)
61. Copper is smelted from ____. (Job 28:2 NIV)
62. Strokes.
63. Apollo's mother.
64. The ____ gave up the dead which were in it. (Rev. 20:13)
65. Hartebeeste.
66. A river went out of ____ to water the garden. (Gen. 2:10)
67. That which ye have spoken in the ____ in closets. (Luke 12:3)

Down

1. To the only ____ God our Saviour. (Jude 25)
2. Let him eschew ____, and do good. (1 Peter 3:11)
3. Salathiel, which was the son of ____. (Luke 3:27)
4. Golden vials full of ____, which are the prayers. (Rev. 5:8)
5. To think (archaic).
6. Dinah the daughter of ____. (Gen. 34:1)
7. The lion shall eat ____ like the bullock. (Isa. 65:25)
8. ____ shall be saved in childbearing. (1 Tim. 2:15)
9. Walk in my ways . . . then I will ____ thy days. (1 Kings 3:14)
10. Indeed (Irish).
11. My days are swifter than a ____. (Job 9:25)
19. ____ gave them bread from heaven to eat. (John 6:31)
21. Might be judged according to ____ in the flesh. (1 Peter 4:6)
24. Behind him a ____ caught in a thicket. (Gen. 22:13)
26. One ____ and filled a spunge full of vinegar. (Mark 15:36)

38

27. ____ took all the silver and the gold that were left in the treasures of the house. (1 Kings 15:18)
28. The God of Israel stirred up the spirit of ____ king of Assyria. (1 Chron. 5:26)
29. Wine for the sake of your stomach and your frequent ____. (1 Tim. 5:23 NASB)
31. Why ____ am I also judged as a sinner? (Rom. 3:7)
33. In whom ____ hid all the treasures of wisdom. (Col. 2:3)
34. Their bows will ____ down the young men. (Isa. 13:18 NASB)
36. Wisdom is ____ high for a fool. (Prov. 24:7)
38. With lies ye have made the heart of the righteous ____. (Ezek. 13:22)
41. Lusts, which ____ against the soul. (1 Peter 2:11)

43. Ain, ____, and Ether, and Ashan; four cities. (Josh. 19:7)
46. Book containing sixty-six books.
48. Now ____ see not yet all things put under him. (Heb. 2:8)
49. California wine valley.
50. Despise not one of these little ____. (Matt. 18:10)
52. This man shall be blessed in his ____. (James 1:25)
54. Portion.
55. And drove all from the temple ____. (John 2:15 NIV)
56. Let us draw ____ with a true heart. (Heb. 10:22)
58. Mother Gynt.
60. Baal-peor, and ____ the sacrifices of the dead. (Ps. 106:28)

39

18

Across

1. The daughter of Phanuel, of the tribe of ____. (Luke 2:36)
5. A tower, whose ____ may reach unto heaven. (Gen. 11:4)
8. The rough ____ is the king of Grecia. (Dan. 8:21)
12. God ____ unto him, to shew unto his servants things which must shortly come to pass. (Rev. 1:1)
13. Artificial language.
14. Put you in remembrance, though ye ___ knew this. (Jude 5)
15. Release.
16. Make thy belly to swell, and thy thigh to ____. (Num. 5:22)
17. Do ye think that the scripture saith in ____? (James 4:5)
18. From so great a death, and doth ____: in whom we trust. (2 Cor. 1:10)
20. He causes his sun to rise on the evil and the good, and ____ rain. (Matt. 5:45 NIV)
21. There was given me a reed like unto a ____. (Rev. 11:1)
22. As for the stork, the ____ trees are her house. (Ps. 104:17)
23. Scatter.
26. Whom we preach, ____ every man, and teaching. (Col. 1:28)
30. For a reward of their shame that say, ____. (Ps. 70:3)
31. All that handle the ____, the mariners. (Ezek. 27:29)
32. Is the iniquity of Peor ____ little for us? (Josh. 22:17)
33. The temple was finished in all its ____. (1 Kings 6:38 NIV)
36. The law is not ____ on faith. (Gal. 3:12 NIV)
38. In the temple, ____ in every house, they ceased not to teach. (Acts 5:42)
39. We do not ____ after the flesh. (2 Cor. 10:3)
40. The merchants of the earth shall weep and ____. (Rev. 18:11)
43. Art thou come hither to ____ us before the time? (Matt. 8:29)
47. American cartoonist.
48. With an high ____ brought he them out of it. (Acts 13:17)

49. Sibbecai the Hushathite, ____ the Ahohite. (1 Chron. 11:29)
50. I will give free ____ to my complaint. (Job 10:1 NIV)
51. He sent forth a dove from him, to ____ if the waters were abated. (Gen. 8:8)
52. Woe to them that are at ____ in Zion. (Amos 6:1)
53. The ____ are a people not strong. (Prov. 30:25)
54. Take thee a great roll, and write in it with a man's ____. (Isa. 8:1)
55. The love of God is ____ abroad in our hearts. (Rom. 5:5)

Down

1. Being such an one as Paul the ____. (Philem. 9)
2. The ____ shall drink of the wine of the wrath. (Rev. 14:10)
3. Thou canst not bear them which are ____. (Rev. 2:2)
4. ____, stay not: for I will bring evil. (Jer. 4:6)
5. She painted her face, and ____ her head. (2 Kings 9:30)
6. By this time there is a bad ____. (John 11:39 NIV)
7. The golden ____ that had manna, and Aaron's rod. (Heb. 9:4)
8. Shall even he that hateth right ____? (Job 34:17)
9. The sons of Judah were Er and ____. (Num. 26:19)
10. Tart.
11. He said, I will not destroy it for ____ sake. (Gen. 18:32)
19. Shorn his head in Cenchrea: for he had a ____. (Acts 18:18)
20. ____, come down ere my child die. (John 4:49)
22. The same also that ascended up ____ above all heavens. (Eph. 4:10)
23. With lies ye have made the heart of the righteous ____. (Ezek. 13:22)
24. I may make ____ gospel of Christ without charge. (1 Cor. 9:18)
25. Unclean for you: the weasel, the ____. (Lev. 11:29 NIV)

26. When he ____ called forth, Tertullus began to accuse him. (Acts 24:2)

27. That which groweth of ____ own accord. (Lev. 25:5)

28. Marrying and giving in marriage, until the day that ____ entered into the ark. (Matt. 24:38)

29. The Spirit of ____ moved upon the face of the waters. (Gen. 1:2)

31. The king was very ____; and Abishag the Shunammite ministered unto the king. (1 Kings 1:15)

34. Moses' brother and Hank.

35. Brought him to an ____, and took care of him. (Luke 10:34)

36. Blessed art thou, Simon ____-jona. (Matt. 16:17)

37. The ____ which were in heaven followed him. (Rev. 19:14)

39. I will therefore that the younger ____ marry. (1 Tim. 5:14)

40. Call me not Naomi, call me ____. (Ruth 1:20)

41. Ram the firstborn, and Bunah, and ___. (1 Chron. 2:25)

42. The body is a ____. (1 Cor. 12:12 NIV)

43. A good ____ bringeth not forth corrupt fruit. (Luke 6:43)

44. Shimei the son of ____, in Benjamin. (1 Kings 4:18)

45. Promontory.

46. Took two milch kine, and ____ them to the cart. (1 Sam. 6:10)

48. Child shall play on the hole of the ____. (Isa. 11:8)

41

19

Across

1. A night and a day I have been in the ____. (2 Cor. 11:25)
5. Their feet are swift to ____ blood. (Rom. 3:15)
9. God created man in his ____ image. (Gen. 1:27)
12. Northern Caucasian language.
13. Take thine ____, eat, drink, and be merry. (Luke 12:19)
14. ____, which was the son of Lamech. (Luke 3:36)
15. Tiber tributary.
16. He has brought Greeks into the temple ____. (Acts 21:28 NIV)
17. The ____ will feed with the bear. (Isa. 11:7 NIV)
18. Was in the ____ that is called Patmos. (Rev. 1:9)
20. Justified by faith without the ____ of the law. (Rom. 3:28)
22. I sharpen my flashing sword and my hand ____ it in judgment. (Deut. 32:41 NIV)
25. Blind, or broken, or maimed, or having a ____. (Lev. 22:22)
26. English tar.
27. I will be his God, and he shall be my ____. (Rev. 21:7)
28. Color changer.
31. The navy of Tharshish, bringing gold, and silver, ivory, and ____. (1 Kings 10:22)
32. He places in the jaws of the peoples a ____ that leads them astray. (Isa. 30:28 NIV)
33. If thou judge the law, thou art not a ____. (James 4:11)
34. Daniel was taken up out of the ____. (Dan. 6:23)
35. A false prophet, a Jew, whose name was ____-jesus. (Acts 13:6)
36. Isaac digged again the ____ of water. (Gen. 26:18)
37. Thou ____ righteous, O Lord. (Rev.16:5)
38. Every ____ of the warrior is with confused noise. (Isa. 9:5)
39. Of Judah, ____, one of the brethren of David. (1 Chron. 27:18)
42. Repent; or ____ I will come unto thee. (Rev. 2:16)

43. A chest and bored a hole in the ____ of it. (2 Kings 12:9)
44. He was manifested to ____ away our sins. (1 John 3:5)
46. He should not ____ long in the place of the breaking forth of children. (Hos. 13:13)
50. Out of whose womb came the ____? (Job 38:29)
51. Shammah the son of ____. (2 Sam. 23:11)
52. The prophecy of this book: for the ____ is at hand. (Rev. 22:10)
53. Hanged about his neck, and he cast into the ____. (Luke 17:2)
54. Both in the flesh, and in the ____. (Philem. 16)
55. They smote him on the head with a reed, and did ____ upon him. (Mark 15:19)

Down

1. ____ shall be a serpent by the way. (Gen. 49:17)
2. ____; because she was the mother of all living. (Gen. 3:20)
3. Hear this, ye old men, and give ____. (Joel 1:2)
4. Who is like thee, glorious in holiness, fearful in ____, doing wonders? (Exod. 15:11)
5. A book written within and on the backside, sealed with seven ____. (Rev. 5:1)
6. The ____, because he cheweth the cud. (Lev. 11:6)
7. Direction: Joppa to Jerusalem (34 miles).
8. Make less sensitive.
9. Christ was ____ offered to bear the sins of many. (Heb. 9:28)
10. Silk, and scarlet, and all thyine ____. (Rev. 18:12)
11. As cold waters to a thirsty soul, so is good ____. (Prov. 25:25)
19. Go and ____ where he is, that I may send and fetch him. (2 Kings 6:13)
21. Behold, there is a woman that hath a familiar spirit at ____-dor. (1 Sam. 28:7)
22. We are ____, when we are weak. (2 Cor.13:9)
23. The harvest of the earth is ____. (Rev. 14:15)
24. All the promises of God in him are yea, and in him ____. (2 Cor. 1:20)

25. Yet what I shall choose I ____ not. (Phil. 1:22)

27. ____, if thou have borne him hence, tell me. (John 20:15)

28. Blockhead.

29. They shall ____ as lions' whelps. (Jer. 51:38)

30. Irish.

32. The heron after her kind, and the lapwing, and the ____. (Lev. 11:19)

33. The LORD ____ all the proud of heart. (Prov. 16:5 NIV)

35. I will hand you over to ____ men. (Ezek. 21:31 NIV)

36. With many of them God ____ not well pleased. (1 Cor. 10:5)

37. ____, thou that destroyest the temple. (Mark 15:29)

38. To drain of fluid.

39. Ancient Greek city.

40. The dust of the earth, and it became ____ in man. (Exod. 8:17)

41. The man who was healed had no ____ who it was. (John 5:13 NIV)

42. The sons of Ram the firstborn of Jerahmeel were, Maaz, and Jamin, and ____. (1 Chron. 2:27)

45. A good while ____ God made choice among us. (Acts 15:7)

47. Send Lazarus, that he may dip the ____ of his finger in water. (Luke 16:24)

48. Pochereth of Zebaim, the children of ____. (Ezra 2:57)

49. They should rest ____ for a little season. (Rev. 6:11)

20

Across

1. For sin, are burned without the ____. (Heb. 13:11)
5. Find grace to help in time of ____. (Heb. 4:16)
9. The vale of Siddim, which is the salt ____. (Gen. 14:3)
12. Hindu caste.
13. Made a whip out of cords, and drove all from the temple ____. (John 2:15 NIV)
14. Put these old rags and worn-out clothes under your arms to ____ the ropes. (Jer. 38:12 NIV)
15. Equal.
16. Now shall Sheba the son of Bichri do us more ____. (2 Sam. 20:6)
17. The LORD smote the Ethiopians before ____. (2 Chron. 14:12)
18. In later times some will ____ the faith. (1 Tim. 4:1 NIV)
20. The truth which is ____ godliness. (Titus 1:1)
22. Pursued the Philistines, and smote them, until they came under Beth-____. (1 Sam. 7:11)
23. A good while ____ God made choice among us. (Acts 15:7)
24. Aloe crystalline.
27. To work.
31. Every night my bed is ____ from my weeping. (Ps. 6:6 GNB)
32. Now Peter ____ without in the palace. (Matt. 26:69)
33. When the ten heard it, ____ began to be much displeased. (Mark 10:41)
34. Behold, I am against you, O valley ____. (Jer. 21:13 NASB)
36. Man's name.
37. Let us ____ and drink; for tomorrow we die. (1 Cor. 15:32)
38. Achar, who brought disaster on Israel by violating the ____ on taking devoted things. (1 Chron. 2:7 NIV)
39. Between us and you a great ____ has been fixed. (Luke 16:26 NIV)
42. Recompensable.

46. My head with ____ thou didst not anoint. (Luke 7:46)
47. ____, which was the son of Seth. (Luke 3:38)
49. He ____ the seven loaves, and gave thanks. (Mark 8:6)
50. I have made you a tester of metals and my people the ____. (Jer. 6:27 NIV)
51. They shall take away thy ____ and thine ears. (Ezek. 23:25)
52. The Pharisees began to ____ him vehemently. (Luke 11:53)
53. We sailed to the ____ of Crete. (Acts 27:7 NIV)
54. Placed on stand.
55. A prophet was beforetime called a ____. (1 Sam. 9:9)

Down

1. Cloak (Spanish).
2. Jezebel said to ____, Arise take possession of the vineyard. (1 Kings 21:15)
3. Variable star.
4. Ye have need that one teach you again which be the first ____. (Heb. 5:12)
5. Know ye Laban the son of ____? (Gen. 29:5)
6. Of ____, the family of the Eranites. (Num. 26:36)
7. People's suffix.
8. Ye might receive ____ by us in nothing. (2 Cor. 7:9)
9. He ____ on the ground, and made clay. (John 9:6)
10. Take thine ____, eat, drink, and be merry. (Luke 12:19)
11. Made the fourteenth day of the month ____ a day of gladness. (Esther 9:19)
19. The Amorites forced the children of ____ into the mountain. (Judg. 1:34)
21. I am glad of the coming of Stephanas and ____. (1 Cor. 16:17)
23. Given to hospitality, ____ to teach. (1 Tim. 3:2)
24. Supposing to ____ affliction to my bonds. (Phil. 1:16)
25. I delight in thy ____. (Ps. 119:70)

Crossword grid with numbered cells: 1, 2, 3, 4, 5, 6, 7, 8, 9, 10, 11 (row 1); 12, 13, 14 (row 2); 15, 16, 17 (row 3); 18, 19, 20, 21 (row 4); 22, 23 (row 5); 24, 25, 26, 27, 28, 29, 30 (row 6); 31, 32, 33 (row 7); 34, 35, 36 (row 8); 37, 38 (row 9); 39, 40, 41, 42, 43, 44, 45 (row 10); 46, 47, 48, 49 (row 11); 50, 51, 52 (row 12); 53, 54, 55 (row 13).

26. Mass.

27. All that handle the ____, the mariners. (Ezek. 27:29)

28. ____, I am warm, I have seen the fire. (Isa. 44:16)

29. The Lord cometh with ____ thousands of his saints. (Jude 14)

30. The light of the body is the ____. (Luke 11:34)

32. The LORD ____ a mark upon Cain. (Gen. 4:15)

35. Ye shall weep and ____, but the world shall rejoice. (John 16:20)

36. The ____ of the Lord will come as a thief. (2 Peter 3:10)

38. The law is not ____ on faith. (Gal. 3:12 NIV)

39. God walking in the garden in the ____ of the day. (Gen. 3:8)

40. The labourer is worthy of his ____. (Luke 10:7)

41. To the sheltered side.

42. ____ your riddle, that we may hear it. (Judg. 14:13 NKJV)

43. Or ____ his jaw through with a thorn? (Job 41:2)

44. Theater seat.

45. Of Jerahmeel were, Maaz, and Jamin, and ____. (1 Chron. 2:27)

48. As it was in the days of ____. (Luke 17:26)

21

Across

1. Whose trust shall be a spider's ____. (Job 8:14)
4. Jacob gave Esau some bread and some lentil ____. (Gen. 25:34 NIV)
8. David dwelt in the ____, and called it the city of David. (2 Sam. 5:9)
12. Adam was first formed, then ____. (1 Tim. 2:13)
13. Get ____ behind me, Satan. (Luke 4:8)
14. The twelfth month, that is, the month ____. (Esther 3:7)
15. The LORD ____ a mark upon Cain. (Gen. 4:15)
16. The magistrates ____ their clothes. (Acts 16:22)
17. When they were put to death I cast my ____ against them. (Acts 26:10 NIV)
18. Perverts, for slave ____ and liars and for perjurers—and for whatever else is contrary. (1 Tim. 1:10 NIV)
20. The dogs came and licked his ____. (Luke 16:21)
21. What mean these seven ____ lambs? (Gen. 21:29)
22. In the clouds to meet the Lord in the ____. (1 Thess. 4:17)
23. As the deer ____ for streams of water, so my soul pants for you. (Ps. 42:1 NIV)
26. By those ____ ye were healed. (1 Peter 2:24)
30. Over you terror, consumption, and the burning ____. (Lev. 26:16)
31. It was impossible for God to ____ (Heb. 6:18)
32. Bind the ____ of thine head upon thee. (Ezek. 24:17)
33. Tautness.
35. He touched the hollow of Jacob's thigh in the ____ that shrank. (Gen. 32:32)
36. As a thread of ____ is broken when it toucheth the fire. (Judg. 16:9)
37. That which groweth of ____ own accord. (Lev. 25:5)
38. Jacob stole away unawares to ____. (Gen. 31:20)

41. He was with the wild ____. (Mark 1:13 NIV)
45. ____, and Dumah, and Eshean. (Josh. 15:52)
46. Man's name.
47. Unclean for you: the weasel, the ____. (Lev. 11:29 NIV)
48. Man's name.
49. They ____ into the bottom as a stone. (Exod. 15:5)
50. Of Zebaim, the children of ____. (Ezra 2:57)
51. He went to the temple to give notice of the ____. (Acts 21:26 NIV)
52. Plural of one.
53. Let patience have ____ perfect work. (James 1:4)

Down

1. An he goat came from the ____. (Dan. 8:5)
2. He that doeth the will of God abideth for ____. (1 John 2:17)
3. Second Greek letter.
4. Scatters.
5. And ____ shall be no more curse. (Rev. 22:3)
6. Odds opposite.
7. They were ____ with the showers of the mountains. (Job 24:8)
8. If you show ____, you sin. (James 2:9 NIV)
9. By this time there is a bad ____. (John 11:39 NIV)
10. A continual allowance given him of the king, a daily ____. (2 Kings 25:30)
11. Very (French).
19. Thou hast defiled my sanctuary with all thy ____ things. (Ezek. 5:11)
20. ____, if thou have borne him hence, tell me. (John 20:15)
22. And ____ the sacrifices of the dead. (Ps. 106:28)
23. Light hit.
24. For inquire, I pray thee, of the former ____. (Job 8:8)
25. His servant Joshua, the son of ____. (Exod. 33:11)

26. If thou doest not well, ____ lieth at the door. (Gen. 4:7)
27. Will men take a ____ of it to hang any vessel thereon? (Ezek. 15:3)
28. The flesh was yet between their teeth, ____ it was chewed. (Num. 11:33)
29. A time to rend, and a time to ____. (Eccles. 3:7)
31. Every mountain and hill shall be brought ____. (Luke 3:5)
34. Charged particle.
35. Odoriferous.
37. Silly.
38. He sojourned in the ____ of promise. (Heb. 11:9)

39. He begged Jesus again and again not to send them out of the ____. (Mark 5:10 NIV)
40. Does a bird fall into a trap on the ground when there is no ____ in it? (Amos 3:5 NASB)
41. The sons of Dishan: Uz, and ____. (1 Chron. 1:42)
42. The sons of Ulla: ____, and Haniel. (1 Chron. 7:39)
43. Lest that which is ____ be turned out of the way. (Heb. 12:13)
44. I ____ up your pure minds by way of remembrance. (2 Peter 3:1)
46. Bear (Spanish).

22

Across

1. Or ____ believe me for the very works' sake. (John 14:11)
5. Mount Sinai, which gendereth to bondage, which is ____. (Gal. 4:24)
9. The sons of Jether; Jephunneh, and Pispah, and ____. (1 Chron. 7:38)
12. Out of him the ____, out of him the battle bow. (Zech. 10:4)
13. Heber, which was the son of ____. (Luke 3:35)
14. Cloth scrap.
15. Sri Lanka vessel.
16. Against (prefix).
17. He casteth forth his ____ like morsels. (Ps. 147:17)
18. ____ held his peace, and answered nothing. (Mark 14:61)
20. There was a marriage in Cana of ____. (John 2:1)
22. Walks by the statutes which ____ life without committing iniquity. (Ezek 33:15 NASB)
26. A great ____ dragon, having seven heads. (Rev. 12:3)
27. God, that giveth to all men liberally and upbraideth ____. (James 1:5)
28. There be quick ____ flesh in the rising. (Lev. 13:10)
30. Tell me, art thou a ____? (Acts 22:27)
34. They gave an ____ translation of God's Law. (Neh. 8:8 GNB)
36. I saw the ____ pushing westward. (Dan. 8:4)
38. Thou shalt bind this ____ of scarlet thread. (Josh. 2:18)
39. The daughter of Asher was ____. (Num. 26:46)
41. A wave of the ____ driven with the wind and tossed. (James 1:6)
43. Direction: Bethlehem to Jerusalem.
44. A papyrus basket for him and coated it with ____. (Exod. 2:3 NIV)
46. Thy lips are like a ____ of scarlet. (Song of Sol. 4:3)
48. The fashion of his countenance was ____. (Luke 9:29)
52. They fled before the men of ____. (Josh. 7:4)
53. We passed to the ____ of a small island called Cauda. (Acts 27:16 NIV)
54. Call me ____: for the Almighty hath dealt very bitterly with me. (Ruth 1:20)
56. Gather the clusters of the ____ of the earth. (Rev. 14:18)
60. Men from Babylon, and from Cuthah, and from ____. (2 Kings 17:24)
61. A river went out of ____ to water the garden. (Gen. 2:10)
62. Of ____, the family of the Eranites. (Num. 26:36)
63. ____, I have no man, when the water is troubled. (John 5:7)
64. Exceeding in ____ attire upon their heads, all of them princes. (Ezek. 23:15)
65. Their princes shall fall by the sword for the ____ of their tongue. (Hos. 7:16)

Down

1. Receiving the ____ of your faith. (1 Peter 1:9)
2. Tai branch.
3. Israel journeyed from the wilderness of ____. (Exod. 17:1)
4. Of Judah, ____, one of the brethren of David. (1 Chron. 27:18)
5. ____ had an army of men that bare targets. (2 Chron. 14:8)
6. The priests are like a ____ of robbers. (Hos. 6:9 GNB)
7. Noah builded an ____ unto the Lord. (Gen. 8:20)
8. An idolater, or a ____, or a drunkard. (1 Cor. 5:11)
9. Seed covering.
10. Let us run with patience the ____. (Heb. 12:1)
11. Shammah the son of ____. (2 Sam. 23:11)
19. Do not ____, my beloved brethren. (James 1:16)
21. Woe to the ____ shepherd that leaveth the flock. (Zech. 11:17)
22. Seth lived after he begat ____. (Gen. 5:7)
23. Woman's name.
24. The name of the ____ is called Wormwood. (Rev. 8:11)

25. His kinsman whose ____ Peter cut off. (John 18:26)

29. Behold, there ____ a man named Zacchaeus. (Luke 19:2)

31. Oweth thee ought, put that on ____ account. (Philem. 18)

32. There was one ____, a prophetess. (Luke 2:36)

33. The city had no ____ of the sun. (Rev. 21:23)

35. The Jews of ____ sought to stone thee. (John 11:8)

37. A certain damsel possessed with a spirit of divination (Acts 16:16)

40. They saw that the fire had not ____ their bodies. (Dan. 3:27 NIV)

42. Let them be turned back for a reward of their shame that say, ____. (Ps. 70:3)

45. His wife hath made herself ____. (Rev. 19:7)

47. Let tears run down like a ____ day and night. (Lam. 2:18)

48. ____, master! for it was borrowed. (2 Kings 6:5)

49. ____ also, who receiveth tithes, payed tithes. (Heb. 7:9)

50. I will ____ your flesh with the thorns. (Judg. 8:7)

51. Dread (Scottish).

55. ____ if the world shall be judged by you, are ye unworthy? (1 Cor. 6:2)

57. ____ the son of Ikkesh the Tekoite. (2 Sam. 23:26)

58. Old horse.

59. Direction: Jerusalem to Jericho.

23

Across

1. South Sea port.
5. Between a run and a walk.
9. Though these three men, Noah, Daniel, and ____, were in it. (Ezek. 14:14)
12. He has cut me off from the ____. (Isa. 38:12 NIV)
13. For the harvest of the earth is ____. (Rev. 14:15)
14. Stand in ____, and sin not. (Ps. 4:4)
15. All (prefix).
16. Cease from sin; beguiling ____ souls. (2 Peter 2:14)
18. Brought in with Jesus into the ____ of the Gentiles. (Acts 7:45)
20. Peter ____ without in the palace. (Matt. 26:69)
21. There came two ____ to Sodom. (Gen. 19:1)
25. Legume.
28. Steep flax.
30. Isui, and Beriah, and ____ their sister. (Gen. 46:17)
31. French cleric.
33. The ____ is turned to his own vomit. (2 Peter 2:22)
35. The ____ is not to the swift. (Eccles. 9:11)
36. Nets.
38. ____ the son of Ikkesh the Tekoite. (1 Chron. 11:28)
40. Behold, I make all things ____. (Rev. 21:5)
41. I can answer anyone who ____ me with contempt. (Prov. 27:11 NIV)
43 Is nigh unto cursing; whose ____ is to be burned. (Heb. 6:8)
45. To the strangers scattered throughout Pontus, Galatia, ____, Asia and Bithynia. (1 Peter 1:1)
50. Pray for those who ____ you. (Luke 6:28 NIV)
53. Thy faith hath ____ thee whole. (Matt. 9:22)
54. His deeds may be made manifest, that they ____ wrought in God. (John 3:21)
55. Repent; or ____ I will come unto thee. (Rev. 2:16)
56. The sons of Ram the firstborn of Jerahmeel were, Maaz, and Jamin, and ____. (1 Chron. 2:27)
57. Below the ____, figures of bulls encircled it. (2 Chron. 4:3 NIV)
58. Moloch and Chiun your images, the ____ of your god. (Amos 5:26)
59. Thou hadst cast me into the deep, in the midst of the ____. (Jonah 2:3)

Down

1. Askew.
2. California Indian tribe.
3. Charged particles.
4. We have sinned, we have done ____. (2 Chron. 6:37)
5. Holy women also, who ____ in God, adorned themselves. (1 Peter 3:5)
6. Tithe of a sen.
7. Protein (Comb. form).
8. Wyoming mountain range.
9. A walking stick—it would break and would ____ your hand. (Isa. 36:6 GNB)
10. I am like an ____ of the desert. (Ps. 102:6)
11. For the ____ is in the land of Assyria. (Isa. 7:18)
17. Provoke not your children to ____. (Col. 3:21)
19. Hear this, ye old men, and give ____. (Joel 1:2)
22. Of ____, the family of the Eranites. (Num. 26:36)
23. The rings of the ephod with a ____ of blue. (Exod. 28:28)
24. And to ____ thee these glad tidings. (Luke 1:19)
25. When the voice was ____, Jesus was found alone. (Luke 9:36)
26. ____, the brother of Japheth the elder. (Gen. 10:21)
27. Man's nickname.
29. ____ sent Joram his son unto king David. (2 Sam. 8:10)

32. Woe to those who ____ evil statutes. (Isa. 10:1 NASB)

34. God is ____ than our heart. (1 John 3:20)

37. I am distraught at the voice of the enemy, at the ____ of the wicked. (Ps. 55:3 NIV)

39. There is one that seeketh ____ judgeth. (John 8:50)

42. Wheat in its place, barley in its plot, and ____ in its field. (Isa. 28:25 NIV)

44. Vaulted roofs.

46. Raisin (Spanish).

47. Ephraim is a ____ not turned. (Hos. 7:8)

48. Their ____ of pleasure is to carouse. (2 Peter 2:13 NIV)

49. Chalice veils.

50. Images of your mice that ____ the land. (1 Sam. 6:5)

51. The sons of Bela; Ezbon, and Uzzi, Uzziel, and Jerimoth, and ____, five. (1 Chron. 7:7)

52. Arphaxad, which was the son of ____. (Luke 3:36)

24

Across

1. There was silence in heaven about the space of ____ an hour. (Rev. 8:1)
5. Salmon begat Boaz, and Boaz begat ____. (Ruth 4:21)
9. Dwelt in the land of ____, on the east of Eden. (Gen. 4:16)
12. Pennsylvania's Great Lake.
13. I will not ____ what man shall do unto me. (Heb. 13:6)
14. Grudge not ____ against another, brethren. (James 5:9)
15. Let us run with patience the ____ that is set. (Heb. 12:1)
16. The devil threw him down, and ____ him. (Luke 9:42)
17. The little book out of the angel's hand, and ____ it up. (Rev. 10:10)
18. The LORD ____ a sweet savour. (Gen. 8:21)
20. Terah begat Abram, ____, and Haran. (Gen. 11:27)
22. Gaelic John.
23. This woman was taken in adultery, in the very ____. (John 8:4)
24. I saw the dead, small and great, ____ before God. (Rev. 20:12)
27. He planteth an ____, and the rain doth nourish it. (Isa. 44:14)
28. God ____ the light, that it was good. (Gen. 1:4)
31. On these two commandments ____ all the law. (Matt. 22:40)
32. The ____ of truth shall be established for ever. (Prov. 12:19)
33. ____ obeyed Abraham. (1 Peter 3:6)
34. Once in the ____ of the world hath he appeared. (Heb. 9:26)
35. Daniel was taken up out of the ____. (Dan. 6:23)
36. ____ the Egyptian, Sarah's handmaid, bare unto Abraham. (Gen. 25:12)
37. Haman was fallen upon the ____ whereon Esther was. (Esther 7:8)
38. Even as a ____ gathereth her chickens. (Matt. 23:37)
39. Let all his ____ be circumcised. (Exod. 12:48)
42. He that sat was to look upon like a jasper and a ____ stone. (Rev. 4:3)
46. Angels, which ____ greater in power and might. (2 Peter 2:11)
47. Was not ____ Jacob's brother? saith the LORD. (Mal. 1:2)
49. Went up to ____, and fetched a compass. (Josh. 15:3)
50. ____ that none render evil for evil. (1 Thess. 5:15)
51. That anointing is ____, not counterfeit. (1 John 2:27 NIV)
52. Pastures.
53. I will give to everyone according to what he ____ done. (Rev. 22:12 NIV)
54. Sailors (slang).
55. The ____ shall drink of the wine of the wrath of God. (Rev. 14:10)

Down

1. Restore all that was ____. (2 Kings 8:6)
2. The children of ____: Uz, and Hul, and Gether. (Gen. 10:23)
3. There were ____ upon man, and upon beast. (Exod. 8:18)
4. Who being past ____ have given themselves over unto lasciviousness. (Eph. 4:19)
5. He, that being ____ reproved hardeneth his neck. (Prov. 29:1)
6. Rosary part.
7. Hear this, ye old men, and give ____. (Joel 1:2)
8. I will ____ the land with your flowing blood. (Ezek. 32:6 NIV)
9. Said unto ____, This is the token of the covenant. (Gen. 9:17)
10. He took Peter, John and James with him and went up ____ a mountain to pray. (Luke 9:28 NIV)
11. The hart, and the roebuck, and the fallow ____. (Deut. 14:5)
19. There is a ____ here, which hath five barley loaves. (John 6:9)
21. For the time is ____ hand. (Rev. 22:10)
23. Child shall play on the hole of the ____. (Isa. 11:8)
24. ____ said, No man, Lord. And Jesus said unto her, Neither do I condemn thee. (John 8:11)
25. To treat hides.

26. Judge not, ____ ye shall not be judged. (Luke 6:37)
27. Their villages were, Etam, and ____, Rimmon. (1 Chron. 4:32)
28. If a man is lazy, the rafters ____. (Eccles. 10:18 NIV)
29. Jephunneh, and Pispah, and ____. (1 Chron. 7:38)
30. In righteousness he doth judge and make ____. (Rev. 19:11)
32. He was ____ as a sheep to the slaughter. (Acts 8:32)
33. Gird thyself, and bind on thy ____. (Acts 12:8)
35. This is a ____ place, and the time is now past. (Matt. 14:15)
36. Let him first cast a stone at ____. (John 8:7)

37. Ye enter, first say, Peace ____ to this house. (Luke 10:5)
38. Pulls.
39. Of Aram; Uz, and Hul, and Gether, and ____. (Gen. 10:23)
40. The children shouting in the temple ____. (Matt. 21:15 NIV)
41. The men that are settled on their ____. (Zeph. 1:12)
42. Moselle river.
43. Their ____ of pleasure is to carouse. (2 Peter 2:13 NIV)
44. The sons of Caleb the son of Jephunneh; Iru, Elah, and ____. (1 Chron. 4:15)
45. Scottish Gaelic.
48. The ____ gave up the dead which were in it. (Rev. 20:13)

25

Across

1. When the dust hardens into a ____. (Job 38:38 NASB)
5. The LORD opened the mouth of the ____. (Num. 22:28)
8. Sodom and Egypt, where ____ our Lord was crucified. (Rev. 11:8)
12. God is ____ of these stones to raise up children. (Luke 3:8)
13. Expression of wonder.
14. Swedish automobile.
15. Considers himself religious and yet does not keep a tight ____ on his tongue, he deceives himself. (James 1:26 NIV)
16. Pochereth of Zebaim, the children of ____. (Ezra 2:57)
17. Judgment also will I lay to the ____. (Isa. 28:17)
18. The Jews made a united ____ on Paul. (Acts 18:12 NIV)
20. To this end I labor, struggling with all his ____. (Col. 1:29 NIV)
22. Upon the great ____ of their right foot. (Exod. 29:20)
23. Love (Scottish).
24. American pub.
27. ____ in peace, be ye warmed and filled. (James 2:16)
31. He is of ____; ask him: he shall speak for himself. (John 9:21)
32. German never.
33. ____ the youngest son of Jerubbaal. (Judg. 9:5)
37. ____, O isles, unto me; and hearken, ye people. (Isa. 49:1)
40. Why make ye this ____, and weep? (Mark 5:39)
41. The suckling child shall play on the hole of the ____. (Isa. 11:8)
42. Floor covering.
45. Hath ____ in our hearts, to give the light. (2 Cor. 4:6)
49. Rejoice ye in that day, and ____ for joy. (Luke 6:23)
50. The battle went sore against Saul, and the archers ____ him. (1 Sam. 31:3)
52. But where are the ____? (Luke 17:17)
53. The Pharisees began to ____ him vehemently. (Luke 11:53)
54. Sir, come down ____ my child die. (John 4:49)
55. The sons of Zebulun; Sered, and ____ (Gen. 46:14)
56. Well (Spanish).
57. ____ me, and deliver me from the hand of strange children. (Ps. 144:11)
58. Soap-frame bar.

Down

1. Call me not Naomi, call me ____. (Ruth 1:20)
2. Knowingly aid.
3. A narrow opening.
4. Called the council together, and all the ____. (Acts 5:21)
5. Awake, harp and lyre! I will ____ the dawn. (Ps. 57:8 NIV)
6. Man's nickname.
7. Fear not, Abram: I am thy ____. (Gen. 15:1)
8. He found them ____ again, (for their eyes were heavy). (Mark 14:40)
9. Like a lion he will leave his ____. (Jer. 25:38 NIV)
10. Paul and Silas prayed, and ____ praises unto God. (Acts 16:25)
11. What shall the end be of them that ____ not the gospel of God? (1 Peter 4:17)
19. Offer the tenth part of a bath out of the ____. (Ezek. 45:14)
21. The day that ____ entered into the ark. (Luke 17:27)
24. ____ Mahal.
25. They would have repented long ____ in sackcloth. (Matt. 11:21)
26. Animal Doc.
28. Go to the ____, thou sluggard; consider her ways. (Prov. 6:6)

Grid (numbered cells):

1	2	3	4	■	5	6	7	■	8	9	10	11
12				■	13			■	14			
15				■	16			■	17			
18			19	■	20	21						
■		22				23			■	■	■	
24	25	26			■	27			28	29	30	
31			■	■	■				32			
33			34	35	36		37	38	39			
■		40				41			■	■		
42	43	44			■	45			46	47	48	
49			■	50	51			52				
53			■	54			■	55				
56			■	57			■	58				

29. The wheat and the ____ were not smitten. (Exod. 9:32)

30. Jesus answering said, Were there not ____ cleansed? (Luke 17:17)

34. There shall no evil ____ to the just. (Prov. 12:21)

35. Soft drink.

36. MYSTERY, BABYLON THE GREAT, THE ____ OF HARLOTS. (Rev. 17:5)

37. The seven days, while their feast ____. (Judg. 14:17)

38. ____-bosheth Saul's son was forty years old. (2 Sam. 2:10)

39. Backbones.

42. In whose hand is the ____ of my wrath! (Isa. 10:5 NIV)

43. Air (comb. form).

44. Cast abroad the ____ of thy wrath. (Job. 40:11)

46. All the depths of the ____ will dry up. (Zech. 10:11 NIV)

47. He called his name ____; then began men to call upon the name of the LORD. (Gen. 4:26)

48. Hid themselves in the ____ and in the rocks. (Rev. 6:15)

51. The sons of Bela; Ezbon, and Uzzi, and Uzziel, and Jerimoth, and ____. (1 Chron. 7:7)

26

Across

1. Deep unconscious state.
5. West Pointer.
9. Adam was first formed, then ____. (1 Tim. 2:13)
12. The daughter of Phanuel, of the tribe of ____. (Luke 2:36)
13. In ____ was there a voice heard, lamentation. (Matt. 2:18)
14. He will silence her noisy ____. (Jer. 51:55 NIV)
15. Sparks' neighbor.
16. On tiptoes.
17. God said unto Noah, The ____ of all flesh is come before me. (Gen. 6:13)
18. I took my staff, even ____, and cut it asunder. (Zech. 11:10)
20. Ye also, as lively ____, are built up a spiritual house. (1 Peter 2:5)
22. Quieting expression.
23. Hindu month.
24. Nor any ____ in the garden of God was like unto him in his beauty. (Ezek. 31:8)
26. In a race run all, but one receiveth the ____? (1 Cor. 9:24)
27. For ____ angel went down at a certain season into the pool. (John 5:4)
29. With a ____ of half a cubit and a gutter of a cubit. (Ezek. 43:17 NIV)
30. Hard or painful struggle.
31. Cornelius said, Four days ____ I was fasting. (Acts 10:30)
32. Judge not, that ____ be not judged. (Matt. 7:1)
33. Cellulose fibers.
34. Shem, Arphaxad, Shelah, ____, Peleg, Reu. (1 Chron. 1:24–25)
35. Compass points.
36. All that handle the ____, the mariners. (Ezek. 27:29)
37. ____ read it in the ears of the king. (Jer. 36:21)
40. Drinking aids.
43. Why make ye this ____, and weep? (Mark 5:39)

44. Ecclesiastical (abbrev.).
46. Where is he ____ is born King of the Jews? (Matt. 2:2)
47. Of Chinneroth, and in the valley, and in the borders of ____ on the west. (Josh. 11:2)
48. Hawaiian island.
49. Geologic vein angle.
50. Pochereth of Zebaim, the children of ____. (Ezra 2:57)
51. Winter vehicle.
52. Norse giant.

Down

1. Engine part (abbrev.).
2. As he saith also in ____, I will call them my people, which were not my people. (Rom. 9:25)
3. ____ the son of Gadi went up from Tirzah. (2 Kings 15:14)
4. Are we trying to ____ the Lord's jealousy? (1 Cor. 10:22 NIV)
5. Is any among you afflicted? let him ____. (James 5:13)
6. Buddhist pillar.
7. Whose ____ was like that of horses. (Ezek. 23:20 NIV)
8. He shall ____ you with the Holy Ghost. (Matt. 3:11)
9. He will make her wilderness like ____. (Isa. 51:3)
10. I am the true ____, and my Father is the husbandman. (John 15:1)
11. The fire devoureth both the ____ of it. (Ezek. 15:4)
19. Digraph.
21. Speak not evil ____ of another. (James 4:11)
23. God shall shoot at them with an ____. (Ps. 64:7)
24. Which shall come upon all the world, to ____ them that dwell upon the earth. (Rev. 3:10)
25. The appointed barley and the ____ in their place? (Isa. 28:25)

26. He has reconciled you by Christ's ____ body through death. (Col. 1:22 NIV)

27. Every man with his staff in his hand for very ____. (Zech. 8:4)

28. ____ yet that he should offer himself often. (Heb. 9:25)

30. Harnessed pairs.

31. Father ____, have mercy on me, and send Lazarus. (Luke 16:24)

33. Peleg lived thirty years, and begat ____. (Gen. 11:18)

34. We have borne the image of the ____. (1 Cor. 15:49)

36. NT's complement.

37. The sons of Onam were, Shammai, and ____. (1 Chron. 2:28)

38. ____ shall be a desolate wilderness. (Joel 3:19)

39. The sons of Lotan; ____, and Homam. (1 Chron. 1:39)

40. Coasted.

41. Where it will turn, join the ____ of Egypt and end at the Sea. (Num. 34:5 NIV)

42. Conditional suffix.

45. Seventeenth letter.

27

Across

1. Heber, which was the son of ____. (Luke 3:35)
5. Doth the wild ____ bray? (Job 6:5)
8. For we ____ not make ourselves of the number. (2 Cor. 10:12)
12. ____, who shall live when God doeth this! (Num. 24:23)
13. The Lord, the LORD of hosts, shall ____ the bough with terror. (Isa. 10:33)
14. Algerian port.
15. No man shall ____ me of this boasting. (2 Cor. 11:10)
16. The flock of Thy possession which dwells by itself in the ____. (Micah 7:14 NASB)
18. The LORD said to ____, Go, take unto thee a wife. (Hos. 1:2)
20. They ____ not, neither do they spin. (Matt. 6:28)
21. Diminutive suffix.
23. The worlds were ____ by the word of God. (Heb. 11:3)
27. I will drive thee from thy ____. (Isa. 22:19)
31. For their ____ hath been to feed cattle. (Gen. 46:32)
32. There was ____ in heaven. (Rev. 12:7)
33. ____ is come salvation, and strength. (Rev. 12:10)
35. Jewish title.
36. Ye ask, and receive not, because ye ask ____. (James 4:3)
39. Sing the song of Moses the ____ of God. (Rev. 15:3)
42. The priest shall not seek for ____ hair. (Lev. 13:36)
44. For the ____ that is in the land of Assyria. (Isa. 7:18)
45. They gave an ____ translation of God's Law and explained it. (Neh. 8:8 GNB)
47. Drone's predecessor.
51. Rained lightly.
55. Having their conscience seared with a hot ____. (1 Tim. 4:2)
56. Bind the ____ of thine head upon thee. (Ezek. 24:17)
57. The Valley of Siddim was full of ____ pits. (Gen. 14:10 NIV)
58. Shall ____ them unto living fountains of waters. (Rev. 7:17)
59. Have they not ____? have they not divided the prey? (Judg. 5:30)
60. He does not ____ away from the sword. (Job 39:22 NIV)
61. Cheers.

Down

1. They are to make: a breastpiece, an ephod, a robe, a woven tunic, a turban and a ____. (Exod. 28:4 NIV)
2. Female voice.
3. S.E. Asian nation.
4. Star's position.
5. Allowance (abbrev.).
6. But now they are blacker than ____. (Lam. 4:8 NIV)
7. Hoax.
8. American monetary unit.
9. Jephunneh, and Pispah, and ____. (1 Chron. 7:38)
10. So they ____ both together: and the other disciple did outrun Peter. (John 20:4)
11. What shall the ____ be of them that obey not the gospel of God? (1 Peter 4:17)
17. He could not draw the dagger out of his belly; and the ____ came out. (Judg. 3:22)
19. "The Lion of God."
22. Time period.
24. Call me not Naomi, call me ____. (Ruth 1:20)
25. God planted a garden eastward in ____. (Gen. 2:8)
26. Go, sell the oil, and pay thy ____. (2 Kings 4:7)
27. On the tops of the hills may it ____. (Ps. 72:16 NIV)
28. But the tongue can no man ____. (James 3:8)
29. Seed coat.
30. We (Latin).

34. Weavest the seven locks of my head with the ____. (Judg. 16:13)

37. Decreased in speed.

38. For he is lunatick, and ____ vexed. (Matt. 17:15)

40. Wherefore art thou ____ in thine apparel? (Isa. 63:2)

41. In him ____ is the love of God perfected. (1 John 2:5)

43. Do not offer to the LORD the blind, the injured or the maimed, or anything with ____. (Lev. 22:22 NIV)

46. Laban gave to ____ his daughter. (Gen. 46:18)

48. He spoke these words while teaching in the temple ____. (John 8:20 NIV)

49. ____ was a just man and perfect in his generations. (Gen. 6:9)

50. Thou shouldest be for salvation unto the ____ of the earth. (Acts 13:47)

51. Postal abbreviations.

52. He smote them ____ and thigh with a great slaughter. (Judg. 15:8)

53. He searches the farthest recesses for ____. (Job 28:3 NIV)

54. O ye ____ bones, hear the word of the LORD. (Ezek. 37:4)

28

Across

1. Bean (Spanish).
5. Total (abbrev.).
8. Legumes.
12. Maple genus.
13. All the hills once cultivated by the ____. (Isa. 7:25 NIV)
14. Hebrew for "to lie with."
15. If I will that he tarry till I come, what is that to ____? (John 21:23)
16. With an high ____ brought he them out of it. (Acts 13:17)
17. He called the name of the well ____. (Gen. 26:20)
18. My lover is to me a cluster of ____ blossoms (Song of Songs 1:14 NIV)
20. Am I not an ____? am I not free? (1 Cor. 9:1)
22. Commercial.
23. I say unto you, ____ your enemies. (Matt. 5:44)
24. The children of Keros, the children of ____. (Neh. 7:47)
27. Strength.
29. Let him seek peace, and ____ it. (1 Peter 3:11)
33. I was ____, because I was naked. (Gen. 3:10)
35. The work of the hands of an ____. (Song of Sol. 7:1 NASB)
36. Tribulation, except they repent of their ____. (Rev. 2:22)
37. Ye do ____, not knowing the scriptures, nor the power of God. (Matt. 22:29)
38. Ye ____ then how that by works a man is justified. (James 2:24)
39. There followed him a ____ of meat from the king. (2 Sam. 11:8)
41. ____ sinful nation, a people laden with iniquity. (Isa. 1:4)
43. There shall arise false ____. (Matt. 24:24)
46. The Lord will come as a thief in the ____. (2 Peter 3:10)
50. As small as the ____ frost on the ground. (Exod. 16:14)
51. For the sky is ____ and lowring. (Matt. 16:3)
53. The Lord also shall ____ out of Zion. (Joel 3:16)
54. Friend (French).
55. Blackbird.
56. Girl's name.
57. Let us not ____ it, but cast lots for it. (John 19:24)
58. Blind, or broken, or maimed, or having a ____. (Lev. 22:22)
59. In the first year of Darius the ____. (Dan. 11:1)

Down

1. Demetrius ____ good report of all men. (3 John 12)
2. Even in laughter the heart may ____. (Prov. 14:13 NIV)
3. Thy statutes have ____ my songs. (Ps. 119:54)
4. Like men condemned to die in the ____ (1 Cor. 4:9 NIV)
5. ____, I am warm, I have seen the fire. (Isa. 44:16)
6. Bad company corrupts good ____. (1 Cor. 15:33 NASB)
7. Musical speed.
8. No chastening for the ____ seemeth to be joyous. (Heb. 12:11)
9. The lightning cometh out of the ____. (Matt. 24:27)
10. From the blood of righteous ____. (Matt. 23:35)
11. I will lay down my life for thy sake. (John 13:37)
19. Gives opinion.
21. Ahimaaz ran by the way of the plain, and ____ Cushi. (2 Sam. 18:23)
24. Be not, as the hypocrites, of a ____ countenance. (Matt. 6:16)
25. African hemp.
26. All things ____ possible to him that believeth. (Mark 9:23)
28. Freud's lowest state.

30. Bro's sibling.
31. ____ hospitality one to another. (1 Peter 4:9)
32. Summer (French).
34. He shall come to be glorified in his saints, and to be ____ in all them that believe. (2 Thess. 1:10)
35. I have given ____ unto the children of Lot. (Deut. 2:9)
37. Hebrew sect.
40. Thus saith Pharaoh, I will not give you ____. (Exod. 5:10)
42. ____ gave Solomon cedar trees and fir trees. (1 Kings 5:10)

43. To scorch.
44. Learn first to shew piety at ____. (1 Tim. 5:4)
45. The earth which drinketh in the ____ that cometh. (Heb. 6:7)
47. Many false prophets are ____ out into the world. (1 John 4:1)
48. Christ sitteth on the right ____ of God. (Col. 3:1)
49. It grew, and waxed a great ____. (Luke 13:19)
52. Jerusalem's splendor, her multitude, her ____ of revelry, and the jubilant within her. (Isa. 5:14 NASB)

29

Across

1. The heart of ____ was perfect all his days. (2 Chron. 15:17)
4. Moses set out with Joshua his ____. (Exod. 24:13 NIV)
8. Their bones, and ____ them in pieces. (Mic. 3:3)
12. Much learning doth make thee ____. (Acts 26:24)
13. You can get a wife for my son from my own ____ and from my father's family. (Gen. 24:40 NIV)
14. Many taken with palsies, and that were ____, were healed. (Acts 8:7)
15. Rejoice over her, thou heaven, and ye holy ____ and prophets. (Rev. 18:20)
17. Ram the firstborn, and Bunah, and ____. (1 Chron. 2:25)
18. Do not sound a trumpet before thee, ____ the hypocrites do. (Matt. 6:2)
19. Heaven is like to a grain of ____ seed. (Matt. 13:31)
21. Then came I with an ____, and rescued him. (Acts 23:27)
24. He that ____ evil hath not seen God. (3 John 11)
25. The appointed barley and the ____ in their place. (Isa. 28:25)
26. Good (French).
27. Famed fabler.
31. MYSTERY, BABYLON THE GREAT, THE ____ OF HARLOTS. (Rev. 17:5)
33. Former archbishop of Canterbury.
34. Flee from the iron weapon, and the bow of ____. (Job 20:24)
35. Now once in the ____ of the world hath he appeared. (Heb. 9:26)
36. Aged (Latin abbrev.).
37. The multitude crying ____ began to desire him. (Mark 15:8)
39. Minor prophet.
40. Lighthouse room with lamp.
43. Type square.
44. The son in law of Shechaniah the son of ____. (Neh. 6:18)

45. The ____ is not above his master. (Matt. 10:24)
50. All things were ____ by him. (John 1:3)
51. Their calls will ____ through the windows. (Zeph. 2:14 NIV)
52. The seventh angel poured out his vial into the ____. (Rev. 16:17)
53. Nebuzar-____ the captain of the guard carried away captive the Jews. (Jer. 52:30)
54. The earth shall ____ to and fro like a drunkard. (Isa. 24:20)
55. They shall ____ his face; and his name shall be in their foreheads. (Rev. 22:4)

Down

1. Medical organization
2. The trees of the LORD are full of ____. (Ps. 104:16)
3. Why make ye this ____, and weep? (Mark 5:39)
4. Praise him for his mighty ____. (Ps. 150:2)
5. Love worketh no ____ to his neighbour. (Rom. 13:10)
6. Evil spirit.
7. Let him seek peace, and ____ it. (1 Peter 3:11)
8. Then took they the body of Jesus, and wound it in linen ____ with the spices. (John 19:40)
9. Brought them unto Halah, and Habor, and ____. (1 Chron. 5:26)
10. An ____ is the tenth part of an ephah. (Exod. 16:36)
11. To await judgment.
16. Let him that heareth ____, come. (Rev. 22:17)
20. Behold, I ____ at the door, and knock. (Rev. 3:20)
21. Took he him up in his ____, and blessed God. (Luke 2:28)
22. They that count it pleasure to ____ in the day. (2 Peter 2:13)
23. For with the same measure that ye ____ withal it shall be measured to you again. (Luke 6:38)

1	2	3		4	5	6	7		8	9	10	11
12				13					14			
15			16						17			
			18			19		20				
21	22	23			24							
25				26			27		28	29	30	
31			32			33						
34					35			36				
			37		38			39				
40	41	42					43					
44				45		46			47	48	49	
50				51					52			
53				54					55			

24. There is a woman that hath a familiar spirit at En-____. (1 Sam. 28:7)

26. Popular girl.

28. The coat was without ____. (John 19:23)

29. Margarine.

30. Payments (abbrev.).

32. Why did the ____ rage, and the people imagine? (Acts 4:25)

33. Their worm dieth not, ____ the fire is not quenched. (Mark 9:48)

35. Thy grandmother Lois, and thy mother ____. (2 Tim. 1:5)

38. Let all things be done decently and in ____. (1 Cor. 14:40)

39. Pochereth of Zebaim, the children of ____. (Ezra 2:57)

40. Eli, Eli, ____ sabachthani? (Matt. 27:46)

41. King ____ the Canaanite, which dwelt in the south. (Num. 33:40)

42. Nothing (Spanish).

43. Class (abbrev.).

46. As soon as ____ heard that Jesus was coming, went and met him. (John 11:20)

47. He was with David at ____-dammim. (1 Chron. 11:13)

48. Glory not, and ____ not against the truth. (James 3:14)

49. Sir, come down ____ my child die. (John 4:49)

30

Across

1. A fig ____ casteth her untimely figs. (Rev. 6:13)
5. The mighty man shall ____ there bitterly. (Zeph. 1:14)
8. No fountain ____ yield salt water and fresh. (James 3:12)
12. And Habor, and ____, and to the river Gozan. (1 Chron. 5:26)
13. Ye tithe mint and ____ and all manner of herbs. (Luke 11:42)
14. To be sailing.
15. Of Sallai, Kallai; of Amok, ____. (Neh. 12:20)
16. Fifty state nation.
17. The Lord God of the holy prophets ____ his angel. (Rev. 22:6)
18. Who ____ their tongue like a sword. (Ps. 64:3)
20. Adam, ____, Enosh. (1 Chron. 1:1)
21. The abomination of desolation, spoken of by ____. (Mark 13:14)
24. Render therefore unto Caesar ____ things which are Caesar's. (Matt. 22:21)
25. I am Alpha and ____. (Rev. 1:8)
26. Thou shalt love thy neighbour as ____. (James 2:8)
30. Musically slower (abbrev.).
31. Who can withstand his ____ blast? (Ps. 147:17 NIV)
32. It was impossible for God to ____. (Heb. 6:18)
33. Build Jerusalem unto the ____. (Dan. 9:25)
36. The LORD said to ____, Go, take unto thee a wife of whoredoms. (Hos. 1:2)
38. There was no room for them in the ____. (Luke 2:7)
39. The life of every person belongs to me, the life of the ____ as well as that of the child. (Ezek. 18:4 GNB)
40. They shall reap the whirlwind: it hath no ____. (Hos. 8:7)
43. His ____ shall be in their foreheads. (Rev. 22:4)
44. That disciple took her unto his own ____. (John 19:27)
45. Cleaning implement.

46. Every man hath received the ____. (1 Peter 4:10)
50. To seek an ____: He will cast lots. (Ezek. 21:21 NIV)
51. The children of this world ____ in their generation wiser. (Luke 16:8)
52. "Dies ____," the Day of Wrath.
53. There ____ up a mist from the earth. (Gen. 2:6)
54. In righteousness he doth judge and make ____. (Rev. 19:11)
55. If then I be a father, where is ____ honour? (Mal. 1:6)

Down

1. All ____ churches shall know that I am he. (Rev. 2:23)
2. God will hear all the words of ____-shakeh. (2 Kings 19:4)
3. Sir, come down ____ my child die. (John 4:49)
4. Insect of Dermaptera order.
5. Others had trial of ____ mockings and scourgings. (Heb. 11:36)
6. Your gold and silver is cankered; and the ____ of them shall be a witness against you. (James 5:3)
7. I therein do rejoice, ____, and will rejoice. (Phil. 1:18)
8. Smashes.
9. As he saith also in ____, I will call them my people. (Rom. 9:25)
10. Neither shall the Arabian pitch ____ there. (Isa. 13:20)
11. The Root of David, ____ prevailed to open the book. (Rev. 5:5)
19. Babylonian god.
20. He does not ____ away from the sword. (Job 39:22 NIV)
21. Co-ed's housing (colloq.).
22. Friend (French).
23. Let down your ____ for a draught. (Luke 5:4)
24. Rise, take up ____ bed, and walk. (John 5:8)
26. Exclamation of disapproval.
27. Or ____ believe me for the very works' sake. (John 14:11)

1	2	3	4		5	6	7		8	9	10	11
12					13				14			
15					16				17			
		18	19					20				
21	22	23					24					
25						26				27	28	29
30					31					32		
33			34	35				36	37			
			38				39					
40	41	42			43							
44				45				46	47	48	49	
50				51				52				
53				54				55				

28. Though ye have ____ among the pots. (Ps. 68:13)
29. How could your servant, a mere dog, accomplish such a ____? (2 Kings 8:13 NIV)
31. Gaelic John.
34. Be ____, O all flesh, before the LORD. (Zech. 2:13)
35. I will not with ____ and pen write. (3 John 13)
36. Jacob sojourned in the land of ____. (Ps. 105:23)
37. Elhanan the son of Jaare-____, a Bethlehemite. (2 Sam. 21:19)
39. The ____ reeds by the brooks. (Isa. 19:7)
40. Come, I will ____ you the bride. (Rev. 21:9 NIV)
41. Ponderous book.
42. The woman shall say, ____. (Num. 5:22)
43. Woman's name.
45. Give unto the priest the shoulder, and the two cheeks, and the ____. (Deut. 18:3)
47. Uzzi, Uzziel, and Jerimoth, and ____. (1 Chron. 7:7)
48. Thou shalt ____ them, and the wind shall carry them away. (Isa. 41:16)
49. Ball stand.

31

Across

1. David sent messengers to ____-bosheth Saul's son. (2 Sam. 3:14)
4. Thou shalt make his ____ to receive his ashes. (Exod. 27:3)
8. Bristle.
12. Do you watch when the ____ bears her fawn? (Job 39:1 NIV)
13. He saith also in ____, I will call them my people. (Rom. 9:25)
14. Having their conscience seared with a hot ____. (1 Tim. 4:2)
15. My head with ____ thou didst not anoint. (Luke 7:46)
16. I will pour out of my Spirit ____ all flesh. (Acts 2:17)
17. The beauty of old men is the ____ head. (Prov. 20:29)
18. Uzziah the king was a ____. (2 Chron. 26:21)
20. Goeth out to Remmon-methoar to ____. (Josh. 19:13)
22. Then was Jesus ____ up of the spirit. (Matt. 4:1)
24. The quiet words of the wise are more to be ____. (Eccles. 9:17 NIV)
28. I saw in the ____ a light from heaven. (Acts 26:13)
31. How is the gold become ____! (Lam. 4:1)
33. The hidden manna, and will give him a white ____. (Rev. 2:17)
34. Drove all from the temple ____. (John 2:15 NIV)
36. He touched his ____, and healed him. (Luke 22:51)
38. Let every man be swift to ____, slow to speak. (James 1:19)
39. He who sows wickedness ____ trouble. (Prov. 22:8 NIV)
41. My speech shall distil as the ____. (Deut. 32:2)
43. DNA component.
44. In wrath you ____ through the earth. (Hab. 3:12 NIV)
46. He will silence her noisy ____. (Jer. 51:55 NIV)
48. Be alway with grace, seasoned with ____. (Col. 4:6)
50. I am not mad, most ____ Festus. (Acts 26:25)
54. Then the children shall tremble from the ____. (Hos. 11:10)
57. Preeminent member.
59. Moses took the ____ of God in his hand. (Exod. 4:20)
60. He that doeth ____ hath not seen God. (3 John 11)
61. I am the LORD, and there is none ____. (Isa. 45:5)
62. Adam was first formed, then ____. (1 Tim. 2:13)
63. Bind the ____ of thine head upon thee. (Ezek. 24:17)
64. And its ____ guard into the western sea. (Joel 2:20 NASB)
65. But ye have made it a ____ of thieves. (Luke 19:46)

Down

1. We know that an ____ is nothing in the world. (1 Cor. 8:4)
2. Silk (French).
3. Find grace to ____ in time of need. (Heb. 4:16)
4. On the Gentiles also was ____ out the gift. (Acts 10:45)
5. Child shall play on the hole of the ____. (Isa. 11:8)
6. Inert element.
7. The name of the one was Bozez, and the name of the other ____. (1 Sam. 14:4)
8. Yea, she ____, and turneth backward. (Lam. 1:8)
9. Do they not ____ that devise evil? (Prov. 14:22)
10. Upon the great ____ of their right foot. (Exod. 29:20)
11. The serpent was more subtil than ____ beast. (Gen. 3:1)
19. He erected there an altar, and called it ____-elohe-Israel. (Gen. 33:20)
21. Roman penny.
23. Men that ____ receive tithes. (Heb. 7:8)
25. A wicked ____ giveth heed to false lips. (Prov. 17:4)

26. Naphtali was Ahira the son of ____. (Num. 10:27)
27. Necks (comb. form).
28. From whence come ____ and fightings among you? (James 4:1)
29. Tally.
30. His parents went to Jerusalem every ____. (Luke 2:41)
32. Much learning doth make thee ____. (Acts 26:24)
35. I am ordained a preacher, and an ____. (1 Tim. 2:7)
37. Sing ye unto her, A vineyard of ____ wine. (Isa. 27:2)
40. Specific dynamic action (abbrev.).
42. Successful one.
45. Submit yourselves unto the ____. (1 Peter 5:5)

47. Art thou better than populous ____? (Nah. 3:8).
49. Distant (prefix).
51. Some of them left of it until the morning, and it ____ worms. (Exod. 16:20)
52. I ____ my master, my wife, and my children. (Exod. 21:5)
53. He will make her wilderness like ____. (Isa. 51:3)
54. They are ____ with the showers of the mountains. (Job. 24:8)
55. Them that were slain; namely, ____, and Rekem. (Num. 31:8)
56. ____, we would see Jesus. (John 12:21)
58. ____ did that which was good. (2 Chron. 14:2)

32

Across

1. ____, and Dumah, and Eshean. (Josh. 15:52)
5. God cannot be tempted with ____. (James 1:13)
9. Sir, didst thou not ____ good seed in thy field? (Matt. 13:27)
12. Do not slacken the ____ for me. (2 Kings 4:24 NKJV)
13. She bound the scarlet ____ in the window. (Josh. 2:21)
14. Stand in ____, and sin not. (Ps. 4:4)
15. Great is Diana of the ____. (Acts 19:28)
17. God said, ____ there be light: and there was light. (Gen. 1:3)
18. The man of wisdom shall ____ thy name. (Mic. 6:9)
19. The "Good King."
20. I ____ a queen, and am no widow. (Rev. 18:7)
22. They will bring a ____ against you. (Ezek. 16:40 NIV)
23. I will be his God, and he shall be my ____. (Rev. 21:7)
24. ____, every one . . . come ye. (Isa. 55:1)
26. I will send My terror ____ of you. (Exod. 23:27 NASB)
29. ____ shall be a serpent. (Gen. 49:17)
30. Achar, who brought disaster on Israel by violating the ____. (1 Chron. 2:7 NIV)
31. Whosoever is ____ of God sinneth not. (1 John 5:18)
32. Behold, I make all things ____. (Rev. 21:5)
33. The record that God ____ of his Son. (1 John 5:10)
34. The two sons of ____, Hophni and Phinehas. (1 Sam. 1:3)
35. The strong shall be as ____. (Isa. 1:31)
36. Are choked with ____ and riches and pleasures. (Luke 8:14)
37. French article.
38. Publicans and sinners ____ also together with Jesus. (Mark 2:15)
39. The coat was without seam, woven from the ____. (John 19:23)
40. ____ not the poor, because he is poor. (Prov. 22:22)
41. I am like an ____ of the desert. (Ps. 102:6)

42. Jephunneh, and Pispah, and ____. (1 Chron. 7:38)
45. Unto the pure all things ____ pure. (Titus 1:15)
47. Book of the Pentateuch.
50. If any man will ____ thee at the law. (Matt. 5:40)
51. Behold, I, ____ I, do bring a flood. (Gen. 6:17)
52. Short cutting stroke.
53. Asked Jesus of his disciples, ____ of his doctrine. (John 18:19)
54. Her ____ have reached unto heaven, and God hath remembered. (Rev. 18:5)
55. Chicks' mothers.

Down

1. Bringing gold, and silver, ivory, and ____. (1 Kings 10:22)
2. Tried to ____ me, but I screamed. (Gen. 39:14 GNB)
3. Even in laughter the heart may ____. (Prov. 14:13 NIV)
4. The ____ that is in the land of Assyria. (Isa. 7:18)
5. Abihail the daughter of ____ the son of Jesse. (2 Chron. 11:18)
6. The seventh angel poured out his ____ into the air. (Rev. 16:17)
7. Set him on his own beast, and brought him to an ____. (Luke 10:34)
8. Now learn this ____ from the fig tree. (Mark 13:28 NIV)
9. Let your speech be alway with grace, seasoned with ____. (Col. 4:6)
10. ____ no man any thing, but to love one another. (Rom. 13:8)
11. His body was ____ with the dew of heaven. (Dan. 4:33)
16. Your feet ____ with the preparation of the gospel. (Eph. 6:15)
21. There was a marriage ____ Cana of Galilee. (John 2:1)
22. They were judged every ____ according to their works. (Rev. 20:13)
23. I ____ a dream. (Dan. 4:5)
24. I ____ chosen you. (John 15:19)
25. Despise not one of these little ____. (Matt. 18:10)

1	2	3	4		5	6	7	8		9	10	11
12					13					14		
15				16						17		
18				19				20	21			
			22				23				24	25
26	27	28				29				30		
31					32				33			
34				35				36				
37			38				39					
		40				41				42	43	44
45	46			47	48				49			
50				51				52				
53				54				55				

26. ____ offered unto God a more excellent sacrifice. (Heb. 11:4)
27. My beloved put in his hand by the ____ of the
door. (Song of Sol. 5:4)
28. ____, the family of the Erites. (Num. 26:16)
29. The heavens shall give their ____. (Zech.
8:12)
30. A Jew . . . ____-jesus. (Acts 13:6)
32. Is it ____ lawful for me to do what I will?
(Matt. 20:15)
33. Stand in the ____ before me for the land.
(Ezek. 22:30)
35. We should leave the word of God, and serve
____. (Acts 6:2)
36. Thy King cometh, sitting on an ass's ____.
(John 12:15)
38. ____ in Christ shall all be made alive. (1 Cor.
15:22)

39. Behold . . . ____ in her womb. (Gen. 25:24)
40. He measured the city with the ____. (Rev.
21:16)
41. The day cometh, that shall burn as an ___.
(Mal. 4:1)
42. Pimple causer.
43. A flattering mouth worketh ____. (Prov.
26:28)
44. He shall suck the poison of ____. (Job 20:16)
45. Maachah the mother of ____ the king. (2
Chron. 15:16)
46. They think it strange that ye ____ not with
them. (1 Peter 4:4)
48. The princes of Midian, ____, and Rekem,
and Zur. (Josh. 13:21)
49. Behold the head of ____-bosheth the son of
Saul. (2 Sam. 4:8)

33

Across

1. ____ ye believed Moses, ye would have believed me. (John 5:46)
4. The ____ that is in thy brother's eye. (Matt. 7:3)
8. My punishment is greater ____ I can bear. (Gen. 4:13)
12. Ye ____ they which have continued with me in my temptations. (Luke 22:28)
13. Abstain from all appearance of ____. (1 Thess. 5:22)
14. Were not the Ethiopians and the Lubims a ____ host? (2 Chron. 16:8)
15. The trees of the LORD are full of ____. (Ps. 104:16)
16. The LORD is my rock, and my fortress, and my ____. (Ps. 18:2)
18. This house was finished on the third day of the month ____. (Ezra 6:15)
20. Was in the ____ that is called Patmos. (Rev. 1:9)
21. He that is called of God, as was ____. (Heb. 5:4)
23. Your moon will ____ no more. (Isa. 60:20 NIV)
25. Rebuild this house of God on its ____. (Ezra 6:7 NASB)
26. Lean animal (Scottish).
27. Warning sound.
30. Direction: Jerusalem to Jericho.
31. In despair, afraid of the roar of the sea and the raging ____. (Luke 21:25 GNB)
32. We passed to the ____ of a small island called Cauda. (Acts 27:16 NIV)
33. His eyes shall be ____ with wine. (Gen. 49:12)
34. Woe to the ____ shepherd that leaveth the flock! (Zech. 11:17)
35. ____ not the sayings of the prophecy. (Rev. 22:10)
36. The people ____ upon the spoil, and took sheep. (1 Sam. 14:32)
37. Him that is ____ to judge the quick and the dead. (1 Peter 4:5)
38. The truth shall make you ____. (John 8:32)

40. No man hath ____ God at any time. (1 John 4:12)
41. To enjoy the ____ of sin for a season. (Heb. 11:25)
44. ____ the son of Ikkesh the Tekoite. (1 Chron. 27:9)
47. Thou art a God who ____. (Gen. 16:13 NASB)
48. Rave's mate.
49. They have no rest day ____ night. (Rev. 14:11)
50. Even darkness which may be ____. (Exod. 10:21)
51. The LORD shall judge the ____ of the earth. (1 Sam. 2:10)
52. ____ thee behind me, Satan. (Luke 4:8)

Down

1. He ____ swallowed me like a monster. (Jer. 51:34 NASB)
2. Sons of Jether; Jephunneh, and Pispah, and ____. (1 Chron. 7:38)
3. They ____; and, lo, the star, which they saw in the east, went before them. (Matt. 2:9)
4. She bare him Zimran, and Jokshan, and ____. (Gen. 25:2)
5. Obey them that have the rule ____ you. (Heb. 13:17)
6. Sesame.
7. Samuel feared to show ____ the vision. (1 Sam. 3:15)
8. ____ filthy dreamers defile the flesh. (Jude 8)
9. He thrust him of hatred, or ____ at him. (Num. 35:20)
10. Shammah the son of ____. (2 Sam. 23:11)
11. ____ begat Kish, and Kish begat Saul. (1 Chron. 8:33)
17. The little foxes, that spoil the ____. (Song of Sol. 2:15)
19. Naphtali is a ____ set free. (Gen. 49:21 NIV)
21. Anna, a prophetess . . . of the tribe of ____. (Luke 2:36)
22. Senior (French).
23. A certain poor ____ casting in thither two mites. (Luke 21:2)

24. ____ was a keeper of sheep. (Gen. 4:2)
26. Caused Solomon to ____ upon King David's mule. (1 Kings 1:38)
27. Would they not leave some ____ grapes? (Jer. 49:9)
28. When ye ____, ye may understand my knowledge. (Eph. 3:4)
29. Because thou didst ____ on the LORD, he delivered them. (2 Chron. 16:8)
31. Lowered him on his mat through the ____. (Luke 5:19 NIV)
35. ____, the smell of my son is as the smell of a field which the LORD hath blessed. (Gen. 27:27)
36. The ruler of the ____ had tasted the water that was made wine. (John 2:9)

37. In the wall of the house he made narrowed ____. (1 Kings 6:6)
38. Shall desire to die, and death shall ____ from them. (Rev. 9:6)
39. The earth shall ____ to and fro like a drunkard. (Isa. 24:20)
40. God shall ____ them strong delusion. (2 Thess. 2:11)
41. Foot/pounds (abbrev.).
42. Scottish mist.
43. ____ greedily after the error of Balaam. (Jude 11)
45. Asahel was as light of foot as a wild ____. (2 Sam. 2:18)
46. I believe that thou ____ the Christ. (John 11:27)

71

34

Across

1. Many of them also which used curious ____ brought their books. (Acts 19:19)
5. Ye have heard of the patience of ____. (James 5:11)
8. ____ and Japheth took a garment. (Gen. 9:23)
12. Traditional knowledge.
13. The serpent beguiled ____. (2 Cor. 11:3)
14. Past tense of heave.
15. The twelfth month, that is, the month ____. (Esther 3:7)
16. Behold a great ____ dragon, having seven heads. (Rev. 12:3)
17. Thy ____ and thy she goats have not cast their young. (Gen. 31:38)
18. The Father sent the Son to be the ____. (1 John 4:14)
20. There is no soundness—only wounds and ____. (Isa. 1:6 NIV)
21. Waters (French).
22. The heron after her kind, and the lapwing, and the ____. (Deut. 14:18)
23. Informers.
26. All the city ____ moved, saying, Who is this? (Matt. 21:10)
29. Affirmative votes.
30. ____ him take the water of life freely. (Rev. 22:17)
31. Sea bird.
32. Look not thou upon the wine when it is ____. (Prov. 23:31)
33. Now Philip was of ____, the city of Andrew. (John 1:44)
35. Said unto ____, Why speakest thou unto them in parables? (Matt. 13:10)
36. Little children, it is the ___ time. (1 John 2:18)
37. They now ____ forth, ye see and know of your own. (Luke 21:30)
40. Whoever ____ the matter separates close friends. (Prov. 17:9 NIV)
43. As small as the ____ frost on the ground. (Exod. 16:14)
44. Scornful exclamation.

45. Fellow of the British Optical Association (abbrev.).
46. He who makes haste with his feet ____. (Prov. 19:2 NASB)
47. I ____ no pleasant bread. (Dan. 10:3)
48. Arm bone.
49. A tree to be desired to make one ____. (Gen. 3:6)
50. ____, which was the Son of Noe. (Luke 3:36)
51. Ogle.

Down

1. ____ for all the evil abominations of the house. (Ezek. 6:11)
2. Nile isle.
3. For three days they ____ in the desert. (Exod. 15:22 NIV)
4. Arranged in a series.
5. The city of the living God, the heavenly ____. (Heb. 12:22)
6. Obey them that have the rule ____ you. (Heb. 13:17)
7. Take up thy ____, and walk. (John 5:11)
8. A certain vessel descending unto him, as it had been a great ____ knit at the four corners. (Acts 10:11)
9. Now, ye rich men, weep and ____ for your miseries. (James 5:1)
10. Newt.
11. There followed him a ____ of meat from the king. (2 Sam. 11:8)
19. Forthwith came there ____ blood and water. (John 19:34)
20. Wondering in himself at that which ____ come to pass. (Luke 24:12)
22. Jesus was born in ____ of Judea. (Matt. 2:1)
23. The valley of Siddim was full of ____ pits. (Gen. 14:10)
24. The light of the body is the ____. (Matt. 6:22)
25. Ye seek me, ____ these go their way. (John 18:8)

26. Capable of being put in writing.
27. ____ the heaven departed as a scroll. (Rev. 6:14)
28. Simon a tanner by the ____ side. (Acts 10:32)
31. At peace.
33. His hand on the wall, and a serpent ____ him. (Amos 5:19)
34. The trees of the LORD are full of ____. (Ps. 104:16)
35. The ____ and his rider hath he thrown into the sea. (Exod.15:1)
37. I will ____ thee my faith by my works. (James 2:18)

38. The sons of Lotan; ____, and Homam. (1 Chron. 1:39)
39. Wherein shall go no galley with ____. (Isa. 33:21)
40. Spices, horses, and mules, a ____ year by year. (2 Chron. 9:24)
41. I wish I could be with you now and change my ____. (Gal. 4:20 NIV)
42. Moselle river.
44. The stone you builders rejected, which ____ become the capstone. (Acts 4:11 NIV)

73

35

Across

1. Hope to the ____ for the grace. (1 Peter 1:13)
4. There in ____ lived a Jew named Mordecai. (Esther 2:5 GNB)
8. To seize suddenly.
12. Recognized value.
13. To ____ that I have loved thee. (Rev. 3:9)
14. Whosoever shall say to his brother, ____, shall be in danger. (Matt. 5:22)
15. Out of whose womb came the ____? (Job 38:29)
16. The sorceress, the seed of the ____. (Isa. 57:3)
18. Like a crane or a swallow, so did I ____. (Isa. 38:14)
20. The paper ____ by the brooks. (Isa. 19:7)
21. Whatsoever they did there, he was the ____ of it. (Gen. 39:22)
22. Israel journeyed from the wilderness of ____. (Exod. 17:1)
23. Carries lightly.
25. They might only touch the ____ of his garment. (Matt. 14:36)
26. Naphtali is a ____ set free. (Gen. 49:21 NIV)
29. Terror, consumption, and the burning ____. (Lev. 26:16)
30. The ____ that was washed to her wallowing. (2 Peter 2:22)
31. We ourselves also ____ sometimes foolish. (Titus 3:3)
32. Sun (Spanish).
33. All that handle the ____, the mariners. (Ezek. 27:29)
34. Do not eat the bread of a ____. (Prov. 23:6 NKJV)
35. Given to hospitality, ____ to teach. (1 Tim. 3:2)
36. Ye pay tithe of ____ and anise. (Matt. 23:23)
37. How right they are to ____ you! (Song of Songs 1:4 NIV)
40. A multitude that kept a ____ feast. (Ps. 42:4 NKJV)
43. The light of the sun shall be ____. (Isa. 30:26)
45. Lod, and ____, the valley of craftsmen. (Neh. 11:35)
46. I have set before thee an ____ door. (Rev. 3:8)
47. Made a serpent of brass, and put it upon a ____. (Num. 21:9)
48. Ye have not ____ resisted unto blood. (Heb. 12:4)
49. Plant cutter bird.
50. O fools, and ____ of heart to believe. (Luke 24:25)
51. He that will love life, and ____ good days. (1 Peter 3:10)

Down

1. Heroic poem.
2. After (German).
3. O Lord, the great and ____ God. (Dan. 9:4)
4. Ray type.
5. Reserved in everlasting chains ____ darkness. (Jude 6)
6. The fathers have eaten ____ grapes. (Ezek. 18:2)
7. Pierce his ear with an ____. (Exod. 21:6 NIV)
8. If they do these things in a ____ tree, what shall be done in the dry? (Luke 23:31)
9. It is a ____ thing that the king requireth. (Dan. 2:11)
10. Perfectly served.
11. The fire shall devour thy ____. (Nah. 3:13)
17. Cut down the tree and ____ off its branches. (Dan. 4:14 NIV)
19. Hand carry.
22. Woe to the women that ____ pillows. (Ezek. 13:18)
23. Which in time past ____ to thee unprofitable. (Philem. 11)
24. I knew a man in Christ above fourteen years ____. (2 Cor. 12:2)
25. Aaron thy brother died in mount ____. (Deut. 32:50)

74

26. One sinner ____ much good. (Eccles. 9:18 NIV)
27. Copper is smelted from ____. (Job 28:2 NIV)
28. Poetic before.
30. It was he which ____ for alms at the Beautiful gate. (Acts 3:10)
31. Under it shall dwell all fowl of every ____. (Ezek. 17:23)
33. Have a matter against any man, the law is ____. (Acts 19:38)
34. I smote you with blasting and with ____. (Hag. 2:17)
35. Like men condemned to die in the ____. (1 Cor. 4:9 NIV)

36. And repaired ____ in the city of David. (2 Chron. 32:5)
37. Musical instrument.
38. D. E. Indies measurement.
39. Hath not the potter power ____ the clay. (Rom. 9:21)
40. Go, wash in the ____ of Siloam. (John 9:7)
41. Arrow poison.
42. Let me pull out the ____ that is in thine eye. (Luke 6:42)
44. Speed (abbrev.).

36

Across

1. ___, and Dumah, and Eshean. (Josh. 15:52)
5. The ____ sitting upon the young. (Deut. 22:6)
8. Action verb suffixes.
12. Put a pillow of goats' ____ for his bolster. (1 Sam. 19:13)
13. ____ the son of Ikkesh the Tekoite. (1 Chron. 27:9)
14. When Paul was brought before ____. (2 Tim. subscr.)
15. To the chief singer on my ____ instruments. (Hab. 3:19)
17. Lest they should fall into the quicksands, strake ____. (Acts 27:17)
18. Cape.
19. Whoever ____ a sinner away from his error will save him. (James 5:20 NIV)
20. The fowls of the air may ____ under the shadow. (Mark 4:32)
23. I will cut off the remnant of ____. (Zeph. 1:4)
25. Called his name ____: then began men to call upon the name of the LORD. (Gen. 4:26)
26. Spare not, ____ thy cords, and strengthen thy stakes. (Isa. 54:2)
30. I took the little book out of the angel's hand, and ____ it up. (Rev. 10:10)
31. Greek transliteration for WORD, as in John 1:1.
32. Military address.
33. Your sins are ____ you for his name's sake. (1 John 2:12)
35. The children of ____ of Hezekiah, ninety and eight. (Ezra 2:16)
36. Freedman.
37. Of the tribe of Ephraim, ____ the son of Nun. (Num. 13:8)
38. My ____ is poured upon the earth. (Lam. 2:11)
41. I will not with ____ and pen write unto thee. (3 John 13)
42. Their ____ of pleasure is to carouse. (2 Peter 2:13 NIV)

43. I know that my ___ liveth. (Job 19:25)
48. Dawn.
49. My heart standeth in ____ of thy word. (Ps. 119:161)
50. No man might buy or sell, ____ he that had the mark. (Rev. 13:17)
51. And Aaron said unto Moses, ____. (Num. 12:11)
52. There was no more ____. (Rev. 21:1)
53. The leaves of the ____ were for the healing of nations. (Rev. 22:2)

Down

1. Expressions of surprise.
2. Unclean for you: the weasel, the ____. (Lev. 11:29 NIV)
3. The sun and the ____ were darkened. (Rev. 9:2)
4. When sin is accomplished, it ____ forth death. (James 1:15 NASB)
5. Whoever ____ a pit may fall into it. (Eccles. 10:8 NIV)
6. What ____ these which are arrayed in white robes? (Rev. 7:13)
7. The prophet is a fool, the spiritual man is ____. (Hos. 9:7)
8. Sennacherib has sent to ____ the living God. (2 Kings 19:16 NIV)
9. Philip, Go ____, and join thyself to this chariot. (Acts 8:29)
10. Watch out for people who ____ and wink at you. (Prov. 16:30 GNB)
11. Suns (Spanish).
16. Born (French).
19. Tatter.
20. Lo, in her mouth was an olive ____. (Gen. 8:11)
21. It vomited Jonah up ____ the dry land. (Jon. 2:10 NASB)
22. Thou art not a ____ of the law, but a judge. (James 4:11)
23. Take ye wives, and ____ sons and daughters. (Jer. 29:6)

24. Simon's wife's mother lay sick of a fever, and ____ they tell him of her. (Mark 1:30)
26. ____ one another. (John 15:12)
27. From whence then ____ it tares? (Matt. 13:27)
28. Foil.
29. Woman's name.
31. Who is a ____ but he that denieth that Jesus is the Christ? (1 John 2:22)
34. A man ____ heads of grain in the Valley. (Isa. 17:5 NIV)
35. Why ____ thou thus after my name? (Judg. 13:18)
37. From the beginning, that we love ____ another. (2 John 5)

38. Tall-growing bean.
39. Asa destroyed her ____, and burnt it. (1 Kings 15:13)
40. Border (Spanish).
41. "Is that your own ____," Jesus asked. (John 18:34 NIV)
43. Vizier.
44. The poor man had nothing, save one little ____. (2 Sam. 12:3)
45. They ____ my path, they set forward my calamity. (Job 30:13)
46. Adam was first formed, then ____. (1 Tim. 2:13)
47. Sheepfold.

37

Across

1. They are not plagued by human ____. (Ps. 73:5 NIV)
5. Matthat, which was the son of ____. (Luke 3:24)
9. One ____ and filled a spunge full of vinegar. (Mark 15:36)
12. The time is come for thee to ____. (Rev. 14:15)
13. Hating ____ the garment spotted by the flesh. (Jude 23)
14. How long will it be ____ they attain to innocency? (Hos. 8:5)
15. Japanese writing.
16. Strokes softly.
17. The heavens shall give their ____. (Zech. 8:12)
18. ____ every man his share, and his coulter. (1 Sam. 13:20)
20. ____ a little wine for thy stomach's sake. (1 Tim. 5:23)
22. They used brick instead of stone, and ____ instead of mortar. (Gen. 11:3 NIV)
23. Most uninhibited.
26. She bare him Zimran, and Jokshan, and ____. (Gen. 25:2)
29. Upon whom thou shalt ____ the Spirit descending. (John 1:33)
30. Neither shalt thou ____ the corners of thy beard. (Lev. 19:27)
31. Of king Nebuchadnezzar king of Babylon, came Nebuzar-____, captain of the guard. (2 Kings 25:8)
32. How often would I have gathered thy children together, as a ____ doth gather her brood. (Luke 13:34)
33. Surely every man is a ____ breath. (Ps. 39:11 NASB)
34. The tabernacle of God is with ____. (Rev. 21:3)
35. To him was given the key of the bottomless ____. (Rev. 9:1)
36. Metrical line.
37. Manifest in the flesh, justified in the Spirit, seen of ____. (1 Tim. 3:16)
39. He who ____ bathed needs only to wash his feet. (John 13:10 NASB)
40. We passed to the ____ of a small island called Cauda. (Acts 27:16)
41. Saith unto him, We have found the ____. (John 1:41)
45. ____ thought she had been drunken. (1 Sam. 1:13)
47. Aminadab, which was the son of ____. (Luke 3:33)
49. Say ye unto your brethren, ____. (Hos. 2:1)
50. They also may without the word be ____. (1 Peter 3:1)
51. ____ obeyed Abraham, calling him lord. (1 Peter 3:6)
52. For we are ____, when we are weak. (2 Cor. 13:9)
53. Is there any taste in the white of an ____? (Job 6:6)
54. Took the ark of God, and brought it from ____-ezer. (1 Sam. 5:1)
55. Tremble, ye women that are at ____. (Isa. 32:11)

Down

1. Irritates
2. ____ was tender eyed; but Rachel was beautiful. (Gen. 29:17)
3. Wool (Latin).
4. To be undaunted by pain or danger.
5. Uzziah the king was a ____. (2 Chron. 26:21)
6. Man's name.
7. Animal doc.
8. Underwrite.
9. Their ____ is strong; the LORD of hosts is his name. (Jer. 50:34)
10. ____ not all these which speak Galilæans? (Acts 2:7)
11. This cup is the ____ testament in my blood. (1 Cor. 11:25)
19. Take thou unto thee an iron ____, and set it for a wall. (Ezek. 4:3)
21. Direction: Joppa to Jerusalem.
23. Marsh.

1	2	3	4		5	6	7	8		9	10	11
12					13					14		
15					16					17		
18			19				20	21				
		22				23				24	25	
26	27	28			29				30			
31				32				33				
34			35			36						
37		38			39							
	40			41				42	43	44		
45	46		47	48			49					
50			51			52						
53			54			55						

24. Sparoid fish.
25. They may have right to the ____ of life. (Rev. 22:14)
26. Daddy's mate.
27. Put him into the garden of ____ to dress it. (Gen. 2:15)
28. ____ earrings, bracelets, veils. (Isa. 3:19 NASB)
29. Folly is ____ in great dignity. (Eccles. 10:6)
32. And wiped ____ feet with her hair. (John 12:3)
33. I have a ____ from God unto thee. (Judg. 3:20)
35. Without faith it is impossible to ____ him. (Heb. 11:6)
36. Roman pledge.

38. College degree.
39. The singers, ____, Asaph, and Ethan. (1 Chron. 15:19)
41. My ____ among the chariots. (Song of Sol. 1:9 NASB)
42. The same is Micaiah the son of ____. (2 Chron. 18:7)
43. Hoard (French).
44. He smote Peter on the ____, and raised him up. (Acts 12:7)
45. Abraham set seven ____ lambs of the flock by themselves. (Gen. 21:28)
46. A meat offering, mingled with oil, and one ____ of oil. (Lev. 14:10)
48. God will hear all the words of ____-shakeh. (2 Kings 19:4)

38

Across

1. From whence come ____ and fightings among you? (James 4:1)
5. The sound of a shaken ____ shall chase them. (Lev. 26:36)
9. ____, she is broken that was the gates. (Ezek. 26:2)
12. Salted.
13. Poker bet.
14. The Amorites forced the children of ____ into the mountain. (Judg. 1:34)
15. Joseph, being ____ years old, was feeding the flock. (Gen. 37:2)
17. Hail, thou that ____ highly favoured. (Luke 1:28)
18. Diminutive.
19. Our competence ____ from God. (2 Cor. 3:5 NIV)
21. The prophecy of this book: for the time is ____ hand. (Rev. 22:10)
22. He that doeth evil hath not ____ God. (3 John 11)
24. Baltic river.
27. It is ____ for thee to kick against the pricks. (Acts 26:14)
28. Is any thing ____ hard for the LORD? (Gen. 18:14)
31. Jonathan was very ____ of David. (1 Sam. 19:1 GNB)
32. Biblical lion.
33. The son of ____, the son of Shamer. (1 Chron. 6:46)
34. I have ____ you with milk, and not with meat. (1 Cor. 3:2)
35. ____, the family of the Eranites. (Num. 26:36)
36. The LORD had respect unto ____ and to his offering. (Gen. 4:4)
37. Sibbecai the Hushathite, ____ the Ahohite. (1 Chron. 11:29)
38. Forty-eighth state.
39. ____ said, Turn again, my daughters. (Ruth 1:11)
42. These are spots in your ____ of charity. (Jude 12)

46. There was no room for them in the ____. (Luke 2:7)
47. I went up to ____ to see Peter. (Gal. 1:18)
50. They were given in marriage, until the day that ____ entered into the ark. (Luke 17:27)
51. The sons of Dishan; Uz and ____. (1 Chron. 1:42)
52. A continual allowance given him of the king, a daily ____ for every day. (2 Kings 25:30)
53. Being.
54. Naphtali is a ____ let loose. (Gen. 49:21)
55. I will ____ you out of My mouth. (Rev. 3:16 NKJV)

Down

1. Stinging insect.
2. To the sheltered side.
3. Rant's companion.
4. Joanna the wife of Chuza Herod's ____. (Luke 8:3)
5. Master, the Jews of ____ sought to stone thee. (John 11:8)
6. Direction: Nazareth to Tiberias.
7. Baal-peor, and ____ the sacrifices of the dead. (Ps. 106:28)
8. He hath ____ up my way that I cannot pass. (Job 19:8)
9. ____ gave names to all cattle. (Gen. 2:20)
10. The ____, because he cheweth the cud. (Lev. 11:6)
11. The ____ are a people not strong. (Prov. 30:25)
16. Let his ____ that he hath hid catch himself. (Ps. 35:8)
20. We are troubled ____ every side. (2 Cor. 4:8)
22. Thou shalt not call her name ____, but Sarah. (Gen. 17:15)
23. Ireland.
24. Is blind, and cannot see afar ____. (2 Peter 1:9)
25. Even the ____ in the field deserts her new-born fawn. (Jer. 14:5 NIV)

26. Whose ____ is destruction, whose God is their belly. (Phil. 3:19)
27. Brought them unto Halah, and Habor, and ____. (1 Chron. 5:26)
28. Bill.
29. Yet offend in ____ point, he is guilty of all. (James 2:10)
30. My head with ____ thou didst not anoint. (Luke 7:46)
33. Markets (Persian).
35. ____ the Tishbite, who was of . . . Gilead. (1 Kings 17:1)
37. Negative prefix.
38. Roman coins.

39. Were there not ten cleansed? but where are the ____? (Luke 17:17)
40. Heareth the word, and ____ with joy received it. (Matt. 13:20)
41. Take heed that ye despise not one of these little ____. (Matt. 18:10)
42. Stored resource.
43. Let him ____ your left cheek too. (Matt. 5:39 GNB)
44. Head (French).
45. Merganser.
48. ____, the family of the Erites. (Num. 26:16)
49. The whole herd of swine ____ violently down. (Matt. 8:32)

39

Across

1. Let us cast ____, that we may know for whose cause this evil is upon us. (Jon. 1:7)
5. Let us run with patience the ____ that is set. (Heb. 12:1)
9. Terah took Abram his son, and ____ the son of Haran his son's son. (Gen. 11:31)
12. The lightning cometh out of the ____. (Matt. 24:27)
13. Babylonian war god.
14. Having the same love, being of ____ accord. (Phil. 2:2)
15. We have seen his ____ in the east. (Matt. 2:2)
16. Take handfuls of ____ from a furnace and have Moses toss it into the air. (Exod. 9:8 NIV)
17. I ____ no pleasant bread. (Dan. 10:3)
18. He touched the hollow of Jacob's thigh in the sinew that ____. (Gen. 32:32)
20. Full of the Holy Ghost and ____. (Acts 6:3)
21. Hunting cry.
23. Direction: Joppa to Nazareth.
24. Honour ____ men. Love the brotherhood. Fear God. (1 Peter 2:17)
27. Direction: Caesarea to Nazareth.
29. Sky, which is strong, and as a molten looking ____. (Job 37:18)
33. Works they do for to be ____ of men. (Matt. 23:5)
35. Girl (informal).
37. Authoritative decree.
38. The same day Pilate and ____ were made friends. (Luke 23:12)
40. They smote him under the fifth ____. (2 Sam. 4:6)
42. Wheat in rows, barley in its place, and ____ within its area? (Isa. 28:25 NASB)
43. Lord, thou ____ God, which hast made heaven. (Acts 4:24)
45. Twentieth letter.
47. He saith unto his ____, "Woman, behold thy son!" (John 19:26)
50. I was brought low, and he ____ me. (Ps. 116:6)
54. Of Zebaim, the children of ____. (Ezra 2:57)
55. Joshua son of Nun, Moses' ____. (Josh. 1:1 NIV)
57. We ____ not make ourselves of the number. (2 Cor. 10:12)
58. I saw the ____ pushing westward. (Dan. 8:4)
59. He was armed with a coat of ____. (1 Sam. 17:5)
60. The LORD is God, and that there is none ____. (1 Kings 8:60)
61. They that ____ whole have no need of the physician. (Mark 2:17)
62. Weaver's reed.
63. Took the ____, and smote him on the head. (Matt. 27:30)

Down

1. The more abundantly I love you, the ____ I be loved. (2 Cor.12:15)
2. Those priests were made without an ____. (Heb. 7:21)
3. Czar variant.
4. You will ____ from the words of knowledge. (Prov. 19:27 NIV)
5. He almost died for the work of Christ, ____ his life. (Phil. 2:30 NIV)
6. Orinoco tributary.
7. Hold that fast which thou hast, that no man take thy ____. (Rev. 3:11)
8. The Son of man is come ____ and drinking. (Luke 7:34)
9. Each one should carry his own ____. (Gal. 6:5 NIV)
10. And went up ____ a mountain to pray. (Luke 9:28 NIV)
11. Let the water ____ with living creatures. (Gen. 1:20 NIV)
19. As the days of ____ were, so shall also the coming of the Son of man be. (Matt. 24:37)
21. I can of mine own ____ do nothing. (John 5:30)
24. He planteth an ____, and the rain doth nourish it. (Isa. 44:14)

25. Passed to the ____ of Cyprus. (Acts 27:4 NIV)
26. Celtic Neptune.
28. Let now thine ____ be attentive to the prayer. (Neh. 1:11)
30. According to the prince of the power of the ____. (Eph. 2:2)
31. What will this babbler ____? (Acts 17:18)
32. Feminine saint.
34. ____ begat Shem, Ham, and Japheth. (Gen. 5:32)
36. Gracefully.
39. The diviners have seen a lie, and have told false ____. (Zech. 10:2)
41. For the ____ that is in the land of Assyria. (Isa. 7:18)
44. The fiery ____ which is to try you. (1 Peter 4:12)
46. Rebuke not an ____, but entreat him. (1 Tim. 5:1)
47. Call me not Naomi, call me ____. (Ruth 1:20)
48. The sons of Eliphaz; Teman, and ____. (1 Chron. 1:36)
49. In process of ____ it came to pass. (Gen. 4:3)
51. I looked, and behold a ____ horse. (Rev. 6:8)
52. Gaelic.
53. This man shall be blessed in his ____. (James 1:25)
56. To live is Christ, and to ____ is gain. (Phil. 1:21)

40

Across

1. ____ nigh to God. (James 4:8)
5. That in the ____ to come he might shew the exceeding riches. (Eph. 2:7)
9. How long is it ____ since this came unto him? (Mark 9:21)
12. Plant cutter bird.
13. Persia today.
14. This ____ knows nothing of the law. (John 7:49 NIV)
15. Bringing gold, and silver, ivory, and ___. (1 Kings 10:22)
16. The princes shall fall by the sword for the ____ of their tongue. (Hos. 7:16)
17. Copper is smelted from ____. (Job 28:2 NKJV)
18. Germanium.
19. Football score (abbrev.).
21. ____ and holy is he that hath part in the first resurrection. (Rev. 20:6)
23. Balak brought Balaam unto the top of ___. (Num. 23:28)
25. How long will it be ____ they believe. (Num. 14:11)
26. Of Zebaim, the children of ____. (Ezra 2:57)
28. A troop cometh: and she called his name ____. (Gen. 30:11)
30. Shall not all ____, but we shall all be changed. (1 Cor. 15:51)
34. I can of mine own ____ do nothing. (John 5:30)
36. Weavest the seven locks of my head with the ____. (Judg. 16:13)
38. It is vain for you to rise up early, to sit up ____. (Ps. 127:2)
39. The thief cometh not, but for to ____. (John 10:10)
41. The gospel which ____ preached of me is not after man. (Gal. 1:11)
43. Many knew him, and ____ afoot thither. (Mark 6:33)
44. ____ sent Joram his son unto king David. (2 Sam. 8:10)
46. Whoever ____ a pit may fall into it. (Eccles. 10:8 NIV)
48. His mouth is full of curses and lies and ____. (Ps. 10:7 NIV)
52. They fled before the men of ____. (Josh. 7:4)
53. ____, thou that destroyest the temple. (Mark 15:29)

Down

1. They sacrifice unto their net, and burn incense unto their ____. (Hab. 1:16)
2. Is this man going to ____ the queen? (Esther 7:8 GNB)
3. Set in order the things that ____ wanting. (Titus 1:5)
4. To what purpose is this ____? (Matt. 26:8)
5. The sun and the ____ were darkened. (Rev. 9:2)
6. If they ____ for a thread, will it help them stand? (Job 8:15 GNB)
7. Enlarge thy baldness as the ____. (Mic. 1:16)
8. Your laws are far from him; he ____ at all his enemies. (Ps. 10:5 NIV)
9. Mattathias, which was the son of ____. (Luke 3:25)
10. If an ox ____ a man or a woman. (Exod. 21:28)
11. Jesse, which was the son of ____. (Luke 3:32)
20. Deliver my soul from the sword; my darling from the power of the ____. (Ps. 22:20)
22. ____ me this day thy birthright. (Gen. 25:31)
23. I will even make the ____ for fire great. (Ezek. 24:9)
24. If the ____ flesh turn again, and be changed unto white. (Lev. 13:16)
26. Thy King cometh unto thee, meek, and sitting upon an ____. (Matt. 21:5)

Across

55. Ye tithe mint and ____ and all manner of herbs. (Luke 11:42)
56. Hindu hero.
58. Ye shall be ____ to quench all the fiery darts. (Eph. 6:16)
60. We ____ great plainness of speech. (2 Cor. 3:12)
61. ____ the Zebulonite died, and was buried. (Judg. 12:12)
62. I will fasten him as a ____ in a sure place. (Isa. 22:23)
63. Lamprey.
64. Exceeding in ____ attire upon their heads. (Ezek. 23:15)
65. Preserve me from violent men, who have purposed to ____ up my feet. (Ps. 140:4 NASB)

27. Behold, Jesus ____ them, saying, All hail. (Matt 28:9)
29. The heaven over you is stayed from ____. (Hag. 1:10)
31. He openeth the ____ of men, and sealeth their instruction. (Job 33:16)
32. Depot abbreviation.
33. Take thee a great roll, and write in it with a man's ____. (Isa. 8:1)
35. The ____ of the fool will overtake me also. (Eccles. 2:15 NASB)
37. Jerusalem, building the rebellious and the ____ city. (Ezra 4:12)
40. Every creditor shall release what he has ____ to his neighbor. (Deut. 15:2 NASB)
42. Keros, the children of ____, the children of Padon. (Neh. 7:47)

45. Found a ship of Alexandria sailing into ____. (Acts 27:6)
47. Breach upon breach, he runneth upon me like a ____. (Job 16:14)
48. He that sat upon him was called Faithful and ____. (Rev. 19:11)
49. White whale.
50. ____ to and fro, and stagger like a drunken man. (Ps. 107:27)
51. Blackthorn fruit.
53. Hawaiian chief.
54. Come over into Macedonia, and ____ us. (Acts 16:9)
57. Simeon; ____ the same man was just and devout. (Luke 2:25)
59. Blessed art thou, Simon ____-jona. (Matt. 16:17)

41

Across

1. Swords flashing, spears gleaming, many slain, a ____ of corpses. (Nah. 3:3 NASB)
5. Took two milch kine, and ____ them to the cart. (1 Sam. 6:10)
9. ____ the son of Ikkesh the Tekoite. (1 Chron. 27:9)
12. To lose (obs. form).
13. Places where David himself and his men were accustomed to ____. (1 Sam. 30:31 NKJV)
14. 100,000 rupees.
15. Puerto ____.
16. Dill herb.
17. The ____ of violence is in their hands. (Isa. 59:6)
18. ____ thou the King? (John 18:33)
20. Peter said, ____, why hath Satan filled thine heart. (Acts 5:3)
22. Edged.
25. Bind them continually upon thine heart, and ____ them about thy neck. (Prov. 6:21)
26. Four days ____ I was fasting until this hour. (Acts 10:30)
27. At thy word I will let down the ____. (Luke 5:5)
29. Hodiah the sister of ____, the father of Keilah. (1 Chron. 4:19)
33. Call me not Naomi, call me ____. (Ruth 1:20)
35. I desire that ye faint ____ at my tribulations. (Eph. 3:13)
37. Zeus' wife.
38. Let us be ____ and self-controlled. (1 Thess. 5:6 NIV)
40. The LORD that delivered me out of the ____ of the lion. (1 Sam. 17:37)
42. Isaac came from the way of the well Lahai-____. (Gen. 24:62)
43. There ____ also many other things which Jesus did. (John 21:25)
45. I will raise up for them a plant of ____. (Ezek. 34:29)
47. He was with the wild ____, and angels attended him. (Mark 1:13 NIV)
51. Naughty figs, which could not be eaten, they were so ____. (Jer. 24:2)
52. Half-way.

53. In the sun ____ of Ahaz, ten degrees backward. (Isa. 38:8)
55. Ammah, that lieth before ____ by the way of the wilderness of Gibeon. (2 Sam. 2:24)
58. Behold, the man is become as ____ of us. (Gen. 3:22)
59. Roof edge.
60. Festive.
61. They lightened the ship, and cast out the wheat into the ____. (Acts 27:38)
62. New testament in my blood, which is ____ for you. (Luke 22:20)
63. Stand by the way, and ____; ask him that fleeth. (Jer. 48:19)

Down

1. Images of your mice that ____ the land. (1 Sam. 6:5)
2. Pochereth of Zebaim, the children of ____. (Ezra 2:57)
3. He ran ahead and climbed a ____-fig tree. (Luke 19:4 NIV)
4. As a ____ hurleth him out of his place. (Job 27:21)
5. Tin coin.
6. St. Columbo's island.
7. There is one ____ to the righteous, and to the wicked. (Eccles. 9:2)
8. Though thou ____ me, I will not eat of thy bread. (Judg. 13:16)
9. ____, the Ahohite. (1 Chron. 11:29)
10. Whosoever shall say to his brother, ____, shall be in danger. (Matt. 5:22)
11. Who had done many ____, he slew two lion-like men of Moab. (2 Sam. 23:20)
19. Ye shall have tribulation ____ days. (Rev. 2:10)
21. To Ittah-kazin, and goeth out to Remmon-methoar to ____. (Josh. 19:13)
22. In ____ was there a voice heard, lamentation. (Matt. 2:18)
23. ____, the son of Nathan of Zobah. (2 Sam. 23:36)
24. I will make Jerusalem heaps, and a ____ of dragons. (Jer. 9:11)
28. I have set her blood upon the ____ of a rock. (Ezek. 24:8)

1	2	3	4	■	5	6	7	8	■	9	10	11
12				■	13				■	14		
15				■	16				■	17		
■		18		19	■	20			21			
22	23			■	24	■	25			■	■	■
26			■	27		28	■	29		30	31	32
33			34	■	35		36	■	37			
38			■	39		■	40		41	42		
■	■		43	■	44	■	45	■	46			
47	48	49		■	■	50	■	51			■	■
52			■	53	■		54	■	55		56	57
58			■	59			■	■	60			
61			■	62			■	■	63			

30. Laid hold upon John, and bound him in prison for ____ sake. (Mark 6:17)
31. In a line.
32. Fire spread from one of its ____ branches. (Ezek. 19:14 NIV)
34. ____, which was the son of Esrom. (Luke 3:33)
36. A papyrus basket for him and coated it with ____ and pitch. (Exod. 2:3 NIV)
39. Along with the workmen in related ___. (Acts 19:25 NIV)
41. Whose trust shall be a spider's ____. (Job 8:14)
44. The sons of Elam; Mattaniah, Zechariah, and Jehiel, and Abdi, and Jeremoth, and ____. (Ezra 10:26)

46. Esli, which was the son of ____. (Luke 3:25)
47. ____, who was among the herdman of Tekoa. (Amos 1:1)
48. They came to Jerusalem at the end of ____ months. (2 Sam. 24:8)
49. He scorned the ____ of killing only Mordecai. (Esther 3:6 NIV)
50. The king of Israel: peradventure he will ____ thy life. (1 Kings 20:31)
54. Laden with sins, ____ away with divers lusts. (2 Tim. 3:6)
56. Peak.
57. The ____ appeareth, and the tender grass. (Prov. 27:25)

42

Across

1. Men of Israel, ____: This is the man, that teacheth all men. (Acts 21:28)
5. A ____ tongue brings angry looks. (Prov. 25:23 NIV)
9. Goliath, of Gath, whose height was six cubits and a ____. (1 Sam. 17:4)
12. Small intestine (comb. form).
13. Upon the great ____ of his right foot. (Lev. 8:23)
14. Book leaf.
15. He that believeth not God hath made him a ____. (1 John 5:10)
16. Their villages were, Etam, and ____. (1 Chron. 4:32)
17. Paul had brought him into the temple ____. (Acts 21:29 NIV)
18. Light carrying device.
20. Bishop's hat.
21. Wrath.
22. Woman's name.
23. They will rest from their ____, for their deeds will follow them. (Rev. 14:13 NIV)
26. Thou ____ of David, have mercy on me. (Mark 10:48)
27. Ancient Hebrew unit of measure.
30. Even as ____ is not mixed with clay. (Dan. 2:43)
31. ____ thine house in order: for thou shalt die. (Isa. 38:1)
32. ____: God hath numbered thy kingdom. (Dan 5:26)
33. Teachers' organization.
34. Noah begat Shem, ____, and Japheth. (Gen. 5:32)
35. When ____ was dead, behold, an angel of the Lord appeareth in a dream to Joseph. (Matt. 2:19)
36. Have they not ____? have they not divided the prey? (Judg. 5:30)
38. ____, I have no man, when the water is troubled. (John 5:7)
39. Therefore am I come baptizing with ____. (John 1:31)
41. In the beginning of the ____ pour out thine heart. (Lam. 2:19)
45. Total.
46. Babylon is taken, ____ is confounded. (Jer. 50:2)
47. Egyptian heaven.
48. Laugh (French).
49. With an high ____ brought he them out of it. (Acts 13:17)
50. Among these nations shalt thou find no ____. (Deut. 28:65)
51. The dust hardens into a ____, and the clods stick together. (Job 38:38 NASB)
52. I therein do rejoice, ____, and will rejoice. (Phil. 1:18)
53. Aquarian star.

Down

1. Paul stood in the midst of Mars. (Acts 17:22)
2. Lamb's pseudonym.
3. The fatness of his flesh shall wax ____. (Isa. 17:4)
4. Appoint him his ____ with the hypocrites. (Matt. 24:51)
5. I may tell all my bones: they look and ____ upon me. (Ps. 22:17)
6. Sewed fig leaves together and made themselves ____ coverings. (Gen. 3:7 NASB)
7. Desire.
8. Whensoever I take my journey into ____, I will come. (Rom. 15:24)
9. He that biddeth him God speed is ____ of his evil. (2 John 11)
10. Shammah the son of ____. (2 Sam. 23:11)
11. Philip, Go ____, and join thyself to this chariot. (Acts 8:29)
19. They do alway ____ in their heart. (Heb. 3:10)
20. ____ blasphemed God because of the plague of the hail. (Rev. 16:21)
22. Just ____, vexed with the filthy conversation of the wicked. (2 Peter 2:7)

23. The ____ of truth shall be established for ever. (Prov. 12:19)

24. Paul, thou ____ beside thyself. (Acts 26:24)

25. Despiteful, proud, ____, inventors of evil. (Rom. 1:30)

26. ____, which was the son of Noe. (Luke 3:36)

28. Lod, and ____, the valley of craftsmen. (Neh. 11:35)

29. For the sky is ____ and lowring. (Matt. 16:3)

31. Be not, as the hypocrites, of a ____ countenance. (Matt. 6:16)

32. The Father of ____, and the God of all comfort. (2 Cor. 1:3)

34. Receive ____ in the Lord, as becometh saints. (Rom. 16:2)

35. The battle went sore against Saul, and the archers ____ him. (1 Sam. 31:3)

37. Pities (obs. form).

38. ____ the father of Bethlehem. (1 Chron. 2:51)

39. How thy garments are ____, when he quieteth the earth. (Job 37:17)

40. Operatic solo.

41. The election hath obtained it, and the rest ____ blinded. (Rom. 11:7)

42. To wander.

43. Fraulein's name.

44. Arrange the pieces, the head, and the ____. (Lev. 1:8 NASB)

46. The ____ went forth, and sought to go that they might walk. (Zech. 6:7)

89

43

Across

1. When he ____, he must believe and not doubt. (James 1:6 NIV)
5. Tin coin.
8. What you sow does not come to life unless it ____. (1 Cor. 15:36 NIV)
12. Two voiced song.
13. Let this mind be in you, which ____ also in Christ. (Phil. 2:5)
14. Lest there be any fornicator, or profane person, as ____. (Heb. 12:16)
15. Neither count I my life ____ unto myself. (Acts 20:24)
16. I wrote them with ____ in the book. (Jer. 36:18)
17. It is better to marry than to ____. (1 Cor. 7:9)
18. Time period.
20. Cans.
21. ____, and Tema, Jetur, Naphish, and Kedemah. (Gen. 25:15)
24. Ear (Spanish).
27. Throat clearing sound.
28. He had dipped the sop, he gave it to Judas ____. (John 13:26)
32. The appointed barley and the ____. (Isa. 28:25)
33. I have been an ____ in a strange land. (Exod. 18:3)
34. Burmese knife.
35. To be taxed with Mary his ____ wife. (Luke 2:5)
37. Father.
38. Wilt thou ____ it up in three days? (John 2:20)
39. Woman, where are ____ thine accusers? (John 8:10)
40. Evil (Latin).
43. Isaac dwelt by the well Lahai-____. (Gen. 25:11)
44. The sons of Judah; Er, and ____, and Shelah. (Gen. 46:12)
45. Why make ye this ____, and weep? (Mark 5:39)

47. As cold waters to a thirsty soul, so is good ____. (Prov. 25:25)
51. Roman liquid measure (abbrev.).
52. Below the ____, figures of bulls encircled it. (2 Chron. 4:3 NIV)
53. The Lord rebuke thee, O Satan; ____ the LORD. (Zech. 3:2)
54. At the name of Jesus every ____ should bow. (Phil. 2:10)
55. Twentieth letter.
56. They profess that they know God; but in works they ____ him. (Titus 1:16)

Down

1. Which of you by taking thought can ____ one cubit? (Matt. 6:27)
2. If any man will ____ thee at the law. (Matt. 5:40)
3. Parrot.
4. The ____ did beat vehemently and immediately it fell. (Luke 6:49)
5. There were ____ boys in her womb. (Gen. 25:24 NIV)
6. Waters gushed out; they ____ in the dry places. (Ps. 105:41)
7. If any of you lack wisdom, let him ____ of God. (James 1:5)
8. He is a ____ to do the whole law. (Gal. 5:3)
9. The sons of Asher; Jimnah, and Ishuah, and ____. (Gen. 46:17)
10. Settle down and ____ the bread they eat. (2 Thess. 3:12 NIV)
11. When they had ____ an hymn, they went out. (Mark 14:26)
19. The name of the beast, ____ the number of his name. (Rev. 13:17)
21. The ____, because he cheweth the cud, but divideth not the hoof. (Lev. 11:6)
22. Plural of here or there (Spanish).
23. Eutychus, being fallen into a ____ sleep. (Acts 20:9)
24. Willow.
25. Frozen.

26. ____ shall judge his people, as one of the tribes. (Gen. 49:16)
28. Fraulein's name.
29. Peculiar (comb. form).
30. Wherein shall go no galley with ____. (Isa. 33:21)
31. For a good work we stone ____ not. (John 10:33)
33. Polynesian expression of surprise.
36. Fruit.
37. Out of darkness, hath ____ in our hearts. (2 Cor. 4:6)
39. An altar with this inscription, ____ THE UNKNOWN GOD. (Acts 17:23)
40. All that behold it begin to ____ him. (Luke 14:29)

41. Heareth the word, and ____ with joy receiveth it. (Matt. 13:20)
42. Country road.
43. Claudius had commanded all Jews to depart from ____. (Acts 18:2)
45. ____ thou he that should come? (Luke 7:20)
46. Shall desire to ____, and death shall flee from them. (Rev. 9:6)
48. Adam called his wife's name ____. (Gen. 3:20)
49. Maimed, or having a ____, or scurvy. (Lev. 22:22)
50. Bent timber.

44

Across

1. Rejoicing, so that the city ____ again. (1 Kings 1:45)
5. Expressions of pleasure.
8. For without are ____, and sorcerers. (Rev. 22:15)
12. Persian prince.
13. The LORD ____ a mark upon Cain. (Gen. 4:15)
14. Follow not that which is ____. (3 John 11)
15. Every ____ that openeth the womb shall be called holy. (Luke 2:23)
16. Jephunneh, and Pispah, and ____. (1 Chron. 7:38)
17. With a spear pierced his ____. (John 19:34)
18. It is high time to awake out of ____. (Rom. 13:11)
20. With decency and propriety, not with ____ hair or gold or pearls. (1 Tim. 2:9 NIV)
22. The Valley of Siddim was full of ____ pits. (Gen. 14:10 NIV)
24. ____, we would see Jesus. (John 12:21)
25. Keep the sayings of this book: ____ God. (Rev. 22:9)
29. The paper ____ by the brooks. (Isa. 19:7)
33. The earth standing ____ of the water and in the water. (2 Peter 3:5)
34. The heron after her kind, and the lapwing, and the ____. (Lev. 11:19)
36. Babylonian god.
37. The presence of the LORD God amongst the ____. (Gen. 3:8)
40. If there be first a ____ mind. (2 Cor. 8:12)
43. Wherein was the golden ____ that had manna. (Heb. 9:4)
45. The name of his city was ____. (1 Chron. 1:50)
46. He that is ____ sin among you, let him first cast a stone. (John 8:7)
50. ____ saith, Let their table be made a snare. (Rom. 11:9)
54. Sons of Mushi; Mahli, and ____, and Jeremoth, three. (1 Chron. 23:23)
55. Because Judas had the ____. (John 13:29)
57. Who ____ record of the word of God. (Rev. 1:2)
58. When Paul was brought before ____. (2 Tim. subscr.)
59. To set at liberty them that ____ bruised. (Luke 4:18)
60. Let God be true, but every man a ____. (Rom. 3:4)
61. To curse.
62. When ye shall divide by ____ the land. (Ezek. 45:1)
63. The LORD shall judge the ____ of the earth. (1 Sam. 2:10)

Down

1. Ye mountains, that ye skipped like ____. (Ps. 114:6)
2. Sons of his brother Helem; Zophah, and Imna, and Shelesh, and ____. (1 Chron. 7:35)
3. I will dry up the streams of the ____. (Ezek. 30:12 NIV)
4. Eubulus ____ you, and so do Pudens, Linus. (2 Tim. 4:21 NIV)
5. ____ was wroth with the seer. (2 Chron. 16:10)
6. Your bones shall flourish like an ____. (Isa. 66:14)
7. Upon her head a crown of twelve ____. (Rev. 12:1)
8. Ye kill, and ____ to have, and cannot obtain. (James 4:2)
9. Roman poet.
10. Andre ____, French writer.
11. Winter vehicle.
19. Expression of contempt.
21. According to the prince of the power of the ____. (Eph. 2:2)
23. The ____, which the LORD God had taken from man. (Gen. 2:22)
25. Yet what I shall choose I ____ not. (Phil. 1:22)
26. Lord, who hath believed ____ report? (John 12:38)

27. Atlas abbreviation.
28. Out of the ____ of the bear, he will deliver me out of the hand of this Philistine. (1 Sam. 17:37)
30. Gera, and Naaman, ____, and Rosh. (Gen. 46:21)
31. Ye have made it a ____ of thieves. (Luke 19:46)
32. If a man is lazy, the rafters ____. (Eccles. 10:18 NIV)
35. Put it upon the ____ of Aaron's right ear. (Lev. 8:23)
38. ____ the Hittite answered Abraham in the audience of the children. (Gen. 23:10)
39. Sow (Scottish).
41. There is a ____ here, which hath five barley loaves. (John 6:9)

42. You will make the camp of Israel ____ to destruction. (Josh. 6:18 NIV)
44. There is Meshech, ____, and all her multitude. (Ezek. 32:26)
46. Travel.
47. He had no ____ that what the angel was doing was really happening. (Acts 12:9 NIV)
48. Semester.
49. Arum plant.
51. O ____ man, that faith without works is dead. (James 2:20)
52. Unto Enoch was born ____. (Gen. 4:18)
53. German articles.
56. ____ thee behind me, Satan. (Matt. 16:23)

93

45

Across

1. He deceived them that ____ received the mark. (Rev. 19:20)
4. Rebellious people, ____ talkers and deceivers. (Titus 1:10 NIV)
8. God is greater ____ our heart. (1 John 3:20)
12. The peaceable fruit of righteousness unto them which ____ exercised. (Heb. 12:11)
13. The way of truth shall be ____ spoken of. (2 Peter 2:2)
14. Were not the Ethiopians and the Lubims a ____ host? (2 Chron. 16:8)
15. The trees of the LORD are full of ____. (Ps. 104:16)
16. There shall come out of Sion the ____. (Rom. 11:26)
18. Came Nebuzar-____, captain of the guard. (2 Kings 25:8)
20. Was in the ____ that is called Patmos. (Rev. 1:9)
21. He that is called of God, as was ____. (Heb. 5:4)
23. The same shall drink of the ____ of the wrath of God. (Rev. 14:10)
25. And rebuild the house of God on its ____. (Ezra 5:15 NIV)
26. I will not deny thee in any ____. (Mark 14:31)
27. Phrase (abbrev.).
30. Direction: Gaza to Jerusalem.
31. Afraid of the roar of the sea and the raging ____. (Luke 21:25 GNB)
32. Passed to the ____ of Cyprus. (Acts 27:4 NIV)
33. His eyes shall be ____ with wine. (Gen. 49:12)
34. Asa destroyed her ____, and burnt it. (1 Kings 15:13)
35. ____ not the sayings of the prophecy. (Rev. 22:10)
36. The people ____ upon the spoil. (1 Sam. 14:32)
37. ____ to judge the quick and the dead. (1 Peter 4:5)
38. The truth shall make you ____. (John 8:32)
40. Being born again, not of corruptible ____. (1 Peter 1:23)
41. To enjoy the ____ of sin for a season. (Heb. 11:25)
44. ____ also the Jairite was a chief ruler about David. (2 Sam. 20:26)
47. When he looks at me, he ____ the one who sent me. (John 12:45 NIV)
48. The Father ____ the Son to be the Saviour. (1 John 4:14)
49. They have no rest day ____ night. (Rev. 14:11)
50. Twenty-seventh U.S. president.
51. Thou shouldest be for salvation unto the ____ of the earth. (Acts 13:47)
52. ____ thee quickly out of Jerusalem. (Acts 22:18)

Down

1. Whosoever loves money never ____ money enough. (Eccles. 5:10 NIV)
2. Jephunneh, and Pispah, and ____. (1 Chron. 7:38)
3. The heaven ____ as a scroll when it is rolled. (Rev. 6:14)
4. She bare him Zimran, and Jokshan, and ____. (Gen. 25:2)
5. Reward her ____ as she rewarded you. (Rev. 18:6)
6. The wheat and the ____ were not smitten. (Exod. 9:32)
7. ____, lama sabachthani? (Matt. 27:46)
8. Father, the Word, and the Holy Ghost: and ____ three are one. (1 John 5:7)
9. If he thrust him of hatred, or ____ at him by laying of wait. (Num. 35:20)
10. Shammah the son of ____. (2 Sam. 23:11)
11. ____ begat Kish, and Kish begat Saul. (1 Chron. 8:33)
17. Neither shall fruit be in the vines. (Hab. 3:17)
19. Do you watch when the ____ bears her fawn? (Job 39:1 NIV)
21. Anna, a prophetess, the daughter of Phanuel, of the tribe of ____. (Luke 2:36)
22. Senior (French).
23. Remain a ____ at thy father's house. (Gen. 38:11)

24. River in Austria.
26. ____ is the gate, and broad is the way, that leadeth to destruction. (Matt. 7:13)
27. You will stand outside knocking and ____. (Luke 13:25 NIV)
28. Christ is the ____ of the church. (Eph. 5:23)
29. Because thou didst ____ on the LORD. (2 Chron. 16:8)
31. Lowered him on his mat through the ____. (Luke 5:19 NIV)
35. ____ that none render evil for evil. (1 Thess. 5:15)
36. Draw out now, and bear unto the governor of the ____. (John 2:8)
37. In the wall of the house he made narrowed ____ round about. (1 Kings 6:6)
38. The king of Israel is come out to seek a ____. (1 Sam. 26:20)
39. Striking a ____ where two seas met. (Acts 27:41 NASB)
40. I ____ you forth as sheep in the midst of wolves. (Matt. 10:16)
41. Time zone abbreviation.
42. Sanctified, and meet for the master's ____. (2 Tim. 2:21)
43. To clear a way for.
45. Asahel was as light of foot as a wild ____. (2 Sam. 2:18)
46. Thou ____ worthy, O Lord, to receive glory and honour and power. (Rev. 4:11)

46

Across

1. The mystery which hath been hid from ____ and from generations. (Col. 1:26)
5. Nebuchadnezzar in his ____ and fury commanded to bring Shadrach, Meshach, and Abednego. (Dan. 3:13)
9. To ____ them that dwell upon the earth. (Rev. 3:10)
12. Call me ____: for the Almighty hath dealt very bitterly with me. (Ruth 1:20)
13. ____ the Canaanite, which dwelt in the south. (Num. 33:40)
14. For all the hills once cultivated by the ____. (Isa. 7:25 NIV)
15. When they are dead shall be unclean, whether it is any ____ of wood or clothing or skin or sack. (Lev. 11:32 NKJV)
16. Abraham ____ two sons. (Gal. 4:22)
17. I forgave thee all that ____. (Matt. 18:32)
18. Spanish preposition.
19. ____ told Jezebel all that Elijah had done. (1 Kings 19:1)
21. ____ knew their thoughts. (Luke 6:8)
22. The ____ is clean. (Prov. 14:4)
23. The labourer is worthy of his ____. (1 Tim. 5:18)
27. My Father, whom you ____ as your God. (John 8:54 NIV)
29. All that handle the ____, the mariners. (Ezek. 27:29)
30. Wherefore ____ apart all filthiness. (James 1:21)
31. Yuri Zhivago's love.
32. The LORD God is a ____ and shield. (Ps. 84:11)
33. Wall recess.
34. Why make ye this ____, and weep? (Mark 5:39)
35. To give light to them that ____ in darkness. (Luke 1:79)
36. ____ that which is evil. (Rom. 12:9)
37. Writer.
39. Irish exclamation.
40. For I through the law ____ dead. (Gal. 2:19)
41. And drove all from the temple ____. (John 2:15 NIV)
42. Have ye not read so much ____ this, what David did. (Luke 6:3)
44. My locks with the ____ of the night. (Song of Sol. 5:2 NASB)
47. He searches the farthest recesses for ____. (Job 28:3 NIV)
48. Ring of light.
50. Said his parents, He is of ____; ask him. (John 9:23)
51. Judah said unto ____, Go in unto thy brother's wife, and marry her. (Gen. 38:8)
52. Nebuzar-____ the captain of the guard. (Jer. 52:30)
53. Trouble ____ yourselves; for his life is in him. (Acts 20:10)
54. In ____ was there a voice heard, lamentation. (Matt. 2:18)
55. Benjamin's ____ was five times so much as any of theirs. (Gen. 43:34)

Down

1. God has ascended ____ shouts of joy. (Ps. 47:5 NIV)
2. With his own blood, suffered without the ____. (Heb. 13:12)
3. How long will it be ____ they believe. (Num. 14:11)
4. There cometh a woman of ____ to draw water. (John 4:7)
5. By faith the harlot ____ perished not with them. (Heb. 11:31)
6. ____, and Dumah, and Eshean. (Josh. 15:52)
7. Leah said, A troop cometh: and she called his name ____. (Gen. 30:11)
8. The children of Gad called the altar ____. (Josh. 22:34)
9. Repent ye: for ____ kingdom of heaven is at hand. (Matt. 3:2)
10. Will a man ____ God? (Mal. 3:8)
11. ____ the dogs under the table eat of the children's crumbs. (Mark 7:28)
17. The heaven over you is stayed from ____. (Hag. 1:10)
20. Not only to believe on ____, but also to suffer. (Phil. 1:29)
21. See that she reverence ____ husband. (Eph. 5:33)
22. Actress Leslie ____.
23. As the lad ____, he shot an arrow. (1 Sam. 20:36)

24. I am ____ and Omega. (Rev. 1:8)
25. Open (Spanish).
26. Colorer.
27. All the trees of the field shall ____ their hands. (Isa. 55:12)
28. Ye ____ men with burdens grievous to be borne. (Luke 11:46)
29. Can there any good thing come ____ of Nazareth? (John 1:46)
32. ____, if thou have borne him hence, tell me where. (John 20:15)
33. Neither shall thy name any more be called Abram, but thy name shall be ____. (Gen. 17:5)
35. ____, which was the son of Noe. (Luke 3:36)
36. There ____ certain men crept in unawares. (Jude 4)

38. Take your ____; go ahead and sleep. (Prov. 24:33 GNB)
39. Like men condemned to die in the ____. (1 Cor. 4:9 NIV)
41. Balak the king of Moab hath brought me from ____. (Num. 23:7)
42. ____ for the day! for the day of the LORD. (Joel 1:15)
43. Beloved, now are we the ____ of God. (1 John 3:2)
44. Thy God, O ____, liveth. (Amos 8:14)
45. Ye know how that a good while ____ God made choice among us. (Acts 15:7)
46. Jesus ____ them, saying, All hail. (Matt. 28:9)
47. Fuegon Indian.
49. Sweet drink.
51. A brother ____ a sister is not under bondage. (1 Cor. 7:15)

47

Across

1. I was at ____, but he hath broken me asunder. (Job 16:12)
5. Lift up the hands which ____ down. (Heb. 12:12)
9. My speech shall distil as the ____. (Deut. 32:2)
12. Thou hast not ____ unto men, but unto God. (Acts 5:4)
13. Spread his tent beyond the tower of ____. (Gen. 35:21)
14. The princes of Midian, ____, and Rekem, and Zur. (Josh. 13:21)
15. Turning the cities of Sodom and Gomorrha ____ ashes. (2 Peter 2:6)
16. It is a ____ thing that the king requireth. (Dan. 2:11)
17. What woman having ____ pieces of silver. (Luke 15:8)
18. Indo-Chinese language.
20. Discourages.
22. My heart standeth in ____ of thy word. (Ps. 119:161)
25. Why make ye this ____, and weep? the damsel is not dead. (Mark 5:39)
27. Hebrew measure.
28. Woman's nickname.
29. Ancient British Isle people.
31. Sons of his brother Helem; Zophah, and ____. (1 Chron. 7:35)
34. The dumb ___ speaking with man's voice. (2 Peter 2:16)
35. Governor of New Haven colony (1638–1658).
37. Charged particle.
38. A Prophet was beforetime called a ____. (1 Sam. 9:9)
40. The law is not going to be lost to the priest, nor counsel to the ____. (Jer. 18:18 NASB)
41. Moses called Oshea the son of ____. (Num. 13:16)
42. Weavest the seven locks of my head with the ____. (Judg. 16:13)
44. German article.
45. Last Spanish queen.

46. The prophecy: the man spake unto ____. (Prov. 30:1)
49. I perceive that in all things ye are ____ superstitious. (Acts 17:22)
51. To the tune of "The ____ of the Morning." (Ps. 22 NIV)
52. I have sworn that the waters of ____ should no more go over the earth. (Isa. 54:9)
54. Your moon will ____ no more. (Isa. 60:20 NIV)
58. O LORD, give ____ to my supplications. (Ps. 143:1)
59. Christ also hath ____ suffered for sins. (1 Peter 3:18
60. Adah the daughter of ____ the Hittite. (Gen. 36:2)
61. The fever left her, and ____ ministered unto them. (Mark 1:31)
62. Jotham ran away, and fled, and went to ____. (Judg. 9:21)
63. Winter vehicle.

Down

1. The two sons of ____, Hophni and Phinehas. (1 Sam. 1:3)
2. Shepham to Riblah, on the east side of ____. (Num. 34:11)
3. Going after strange flesh, are ____ forth for an example, suffering the vengeance. (Jude 7)
4. I am faint: therefore was his name called ____. (Gen. 25:30)
5. ____ had a quarrel against him. (Mark 6:19)
6. Woman's name.
7. Mary took about a pint of pure ____. (John 12:3 NIV)
8. They knew all that his father was a ____. (Acts 16:3)
9. He shall pay as the judges ____. (Exod. 21:22)
10. To whom the mist of darkness is reserved for ____. (2 Peter 2:17)
11. He who ____ souls is wise. (Prov. 7:8 NIV)
19. Is this man going to ____ the queen? (Esther 7:8 GNB)
21. ____ sent Joram his son unto king David. (2 Sam. 8:10)

1	2	3	4		5	6	7	8		9	10	11
12					13					14		
15					16					17		
			18	19			20		21			
22	23	24		25		26		27				
28				29			30		31		32	33
34				35				36		37		
38			39		40					41		
		42		43		44			45			
46	47			48		49		50				
51				52		53			54	55	56	57
58				59				60				
61				62				63				

22. ____ for all the evil abominations of the house of Israel! (Ezek. 6:11)

23. Him that cometh to me I will in no ____ cast out. (John 6:37)

24. As Isaiah says ____; "He has blinded their eyes." (John 12:39–40 NIV)

26. Group of eight.

30. Gog and Magog, to gather them ____ to battle. (Rev. 20:8)

32. Verb's complement.

33. There was one ____, a prophetess. (Luke 2:36)

36. When Paul was brought before ____. (2 Tim. subscr.)

39. Nathan the prophet, and Shimei, and ____. (1 Kings 1:8)

43. Ishbi-____, which was of the sons of the giant. (2 Sam. 21:16)

46. March 15th.

47. The son of Eliel, the son of ____. (1 Chron. 6:34)

48. Seeing a ____ fig tree by the road. (Matt. 21:19 NASB)

50. Cancel any debt your brother ____ you. (Deut. 15:3 NIV)

53. Double fault's opposite.

55. Ye are ____ the children of light. (1 Thess. 5:5)

56. Until the day that ____ entered into the ark. (Luke 17:27)

57. What shall the ____ be of them that obey not the gospel? (1 Peter 4:17)

48

Across

1. Scottish fog.
4. I will cut down the ____ cedars. (Isa. 37:24)
8. Ramachandra's wife.
12. She hath also conceived a son in her old ____. (Luke 1:36)
13. Oil (comb. form).
14. ____ lived ninety years, and begat Cainan. (Gen. 5:9)
15. A ____ caught in a thicket by his horns. (Gen. 22:13)
16. As he was ____, he taught them. (Mark 10:1)
17. Were there not ten cleansed? but where are the ____? (Luke 17:17)
18. "Go to bed and ____ to be ill," Jonadab said. (2 Sam. 13:5 NIV)
20. Whosoever will, let him take the ____ of life freely. (Rev. 22:17)
21. Let him that stole steal no ____. (Eph. 4:28)
22. After her kind, and the lapwing, and the ____. (Deut. 14:18)
23. Priests (French).
25. They wandered in ____, and in mountains. (Heb. 11:38)
29. If any man will ____ thee at the law. (Matt. 5:40)
30. Jerusalem, building the rebellious and the ____ city. (Ezra 4:12)
31. Abraham set seven ____ lambs of the flock by themselves. (Gen. 21:28)
32. Was not ____ our father justified by works? (James 2:21)
35. Alpine dweller.
37. Brick instead of stone, and ____ instead of mortar. (Gen. 11:3 NIV)
38. With the ____ of my feet have I dried up all the rivers. (Isa. 37:25)
39. ____ is deceptive, and beauty is fleeting. (Prov. 31:30 NIV)
42. Yet you yourself ____ the law by commanding that I be struck. (Acts 23:3 NIV)
45. The Philistines saw that their ____ was dead. (1 Sam. 17:51 NIV)
46. His meat was locusts and ____ honey. (Matt. 3:4)
47. There is a ____ here, which hath five barley loaves. (John 6:9)
48. Count.
49. Elliptical.
50. Sir, come down ____ my child die. (John 4:49)
51. Affirmative answer.
52. For my yoke is ____, and my burden is light. (Matt. 11:30)
53. Daniel was taken up out of the ____. (Dan. 6:23)

Down

1. My bowels shall sound like an ____. (Isa. 16:11)
2. For this ____ is mount Sinai. (Gal. 4:25)
3. Their sins and their iniquities will I ____ no more. (Heb. 8:12)
4. Uzziah built ____ in Jerusalem. (2 Chron. 26:9)
5. It is not good that the man should be ____. (Gen. 2:18)
6. Friend, ____ me three loaves. (Luke 11:5)
7. Thus were both the daughters of ____ with child. (Gen. 19:36)
8. Called the council together, and all the ____. (Acts 5:21)
9. Initial (abbrev.).
10. How I wish I could be with you now and change my ____. (Gal. 4:20 NIV)
11. The daughter of Phanuel, of the tribe of ____. (Luke 2:36)
19. Upon the great ____ of their right foot. (Exod. 29:20)
20. Titus, who ____ with me, being a Greek. (Gal. 2:3)
22. Take up thy ____, and walk? (John 5:12)
23. Roboam begat Abia; and Abia begat ____. (Matt. 1:7)
24. Boy.
25. It shall be seven days under the ____. (Lev. 22:27)
26. When his glory shall be ____, ye may be glad. (1 Peter 4:13)

27. Hath five barley loaves, and _____ small fishes. (John 6:9)
28. Our brother Timothy is ____ at liberty. (Heb. 13:23)
30. A false prophet, a Jew, whose name was ____-jesus. (Acts 13:6)
33. And ____, Shophan, and Jaazer, and Jogbehah. (Num. 32:35)
34. Wondrous works in the land of ____. (Ps. 106:22)
35. All things which were dainty and ____ are departed from thee. (Rev. 18:14)
36. Jesus Christ his Son cleanseth us from ____ sin. (1 John 1:7)
38. Judas and ____, being prophets also themselves. (Acts 15:32)
39. Red root dye.
40. For ____ have we no continuing city. (Heb. 13:14)
41. Jesus was in the temple ____ walking. (John 10:23 NIV)
42. "Live long!"
43. The devil threw him down, and ____ him. (Luke 9:42)
44. The land of Nod, on the east of ____. (Gen. 4:16)
46. ____ unto the world because of offences! (Matt. 18:7)

49

Across

1. Say ye unto your brethren, ____. (Hos. 2:1)
5. Before.
8. ____, the family of the Arodites. (Num. 26:17)
12. I have ____ God face to face. (Gen. 32:30)
13. So fight I, not as one that beateth the ____. (1 Cor. 9:26)
14. Streaky.
15. Cupid.
16. Clamber hurriedly.
18. Say again.
20. Cobalt.
21. And ____ the lamp of God went out in the temple. (1 Sam. 3:3)
22. Mary, of whom was born Jesus, who is called ____. (Matt. 1:16)
26. You yourselves ____ and do wrong. (1 Cor. 6:8 NIV)
29. Whosoever loveth and maketh a ____. (Rev. 22:15)
30. Widemouthed container.
31. A sacrifice of peace offering, if he offer it of the ____. (Lev. 3:1)
32. French pronoun.
33. Scholarly book.
34. I have broken the ____ of Pharaoh. (Ezek. 30:21)
35. These things ____ good and profitable unto men. (Titus 3:8)
36. The hare, and the ____. (Deut. 14:7)
37. Everyone held that John ____ was a prophet. (Mark 11:32 NIV)
39. Honorable (abbrev.).
40. Your faith ____ spoken of throughout the whole world. (Rom. 1:8)
41. Build Jerusalem unto the ____. (Dan. 9:25)
45. The LORD will ____ their secret parts. (Isa. 3:17)
49. The Pharisees began to ____ him vehemently. (Luke 11:53)
50. He called the name of the well ____. (Gen. 26:20)
51. Lod, and ____, the valley of craftsmen. (Neh. 11:35)
52. Were as swift as the ____ upon the mountains. (1 Chron. 12:8)
53. Dampens.
54. To marry.
55. All the ____ of the world shall remember and turn. (Ps. 22:27)

Down

1. Phanuel, of the tribe of ____. (Luke 2:36)
2. Stop judging by ____ appearances. (John 7:24 NIV)
3. Indian farmers.
4. Took one of his ribs, and closed up the flesh ____ thereof. (Gen. 2:21)
5. Isaiah told the king's attendants to put on his boil a ____ made of figs. (2 Kings 20:7 GNB)
6. Aquatic cereal grass.
7. They ____ in vision, they stumble in judgment. (Isa. 28:7)
8. Put on the full ____ of God. (Eph. 6:11 NIV)
9. ____ not the poor, because he is poor. (Prov. 22:22)
10. The screech ____ also shall rest there. (Isa. 34:14)
11. Coloring agent.
17. Even in laughter the heart may ____. (Prov. 14:13 NIV)
19. ____ thou only a stranger in Jerusalem? (Luke 24:18)
22. Saul the son of ____, a man of the tribe. (Acts 13:21)
23. They smote ____. (2 Chron. 16:4)
24. The ____ is Hebron. (Gen. 23:2)
25. Side of a domino.
26. Scorch.
27. The time of your sojourning ____ in fear. (1 Peter 1:17)
28. Woman's name.
29. We sailed to the ____ of Crete. (Acts 27:7 NIV)

32. The stones would immediately ____ out. (Luke 19:40)

33. Monk's shaven crown.

35. Our gospel came not unto you in word only, but ____ in power, and in the Holy Ghost. (1 Thess. 1:5)

36. We put out to sea and sailed straight to ____. (Acts 21:1 NIV)

38. As an ox ____ up the grass of the field. (Num. 22:4 NIV)

39. Manaen, which had been brought up with ____ the tetrarch. (Acts 13:1)

41. ____: God hath numbered thy kingdom. (Dan. 5:26)

42. They came unto the ____ gate that leadeth unto the city. (Acts 12:10)

43. Being such an one as Paul the ____. (Philem. 9)

44. Pianist Myra ____.

45. Like a cloud of ____ in the heat of harvest. (Isa. 18:4)

46. Verbal suffix.

47. Plant pleasant plants, and shalt ____ it with strange slips. (Isa. 17:10)

48. We have four men which have a ____ on them. (Acts 21:23)

103

50

Across

1. ____ is my washpot. (Ps. 108:9)
5. Wherefore is it that thou dost ____ after my name? (Gen. 32:29)
8. For their welfare, let it become a ____. (Ps. 69:22)
12. Shallowest Great Lake.
13. Naphtali is a ____ set free that bears beautiful fawns. (Gen. 49:21 NIV)
14. Behold, a greater than Jonas is ____. (Matt. 12:41)
15. They are hid in the earth in the midst of my ____. (Josh. 7:21)
16. Stand in ____, and sin not. (Ps. 4:4)
17. The Jews should come back ____ his own head. (Esther 9:25 NIV)
18. Wondrous works in the land of ____. (Ps. 106:22)
20. I have not hastened from being a ____. (Jer. 17:16)
22. Ishmael, Abraham's son, whom ____ the Egyptian, Sarah's handmaid, bare. (Gen. 25:12)
25. To father.
26. Yet I am not ____, because the Father is with me. (John 16:32)
27. Go to the ____, thou sluggard; consider her ways. (Prov. 6:6)
28. He cannot stand; his end ____ come. (Mark 3:26 NIV)
31. For ____ deceivers are entered into the world. (2 John 7)
32. I had to pay a ____ price for my citizenship. (Acts 22:28 NIV)
33. ___ hath Esaias prophesied of you hypocrites. (Mark 7:6)
34. Verbal suffix.
35. How ____ he love God whom he hath not seen? (1 John 4:20)
36. Beware of ____ prophets, which come to you in sheep's clothing. (Matt. 7:15)
37. Then shall the lame man leap as an ____. (Isa. 35:6)
38. For that which I do I ____ not. (Rom. 7:15)
39. Lord, who hath believed our ____? (John 12:38)

42. There was seen in his temple the ____ of his testament. (Rev. 11:19)
43. Ye ask amiss, that ye may consume it ____ your lusts. (James 4:3)
44. Their lives ____ away in their mothers' arms. (Lam. 2:12 NIV)
46. The ____ unto Paphos, they found a certain sorcerer. (Acts 13:6)
50. His vaulted ____ over the earth. (Amos 9:6 NASB)
51. The ____, which the LORD God had taken from man. (Gen. 2:22)
52. Inert element.
53. Sent me from Kadesh-barnea to ____ out the land. (Josh. 14:7)
54. Musical direction.
55. She opened not the ____ for gladness. (Acts 12:14)

Down

1. Falling into a place where two seas ____. (Acts 27:41)
2. I have made you a tester of metals and my people the ____. (Jer. 6:27 NIV)
3. Their villages were, Etam, and ____, Rimmon. (1 Chron. 4:32)
4. A certain man was sick, named Lazarus, of ____. (John 11:1)
5. As in ____ all die, even so in Christ shall all be made alive. (1 Cor. 15:22)
6. Reaping that I did not ____. (Luke 19:22)
7. To the will of God commit the ____ of their souls. (1 Peter 4:19)
8. Except ____ days should be shortened. (Matt. 24:22)
9. The veil of the temple was ____ in the midst. (Luke 23:45)
10. Bread (comb. form).
11. They have beguiled you in the matter of ____. (Num. 25:18)
19. In whom ____ hid all the treasures of wisdom. (Col. 2:3)
21. Thou ____ my beloved Son. (Mark 1:11)
22. Hooks.

23. ____ for all the evil abominations of the house of Israel! (Ezek. 6:11)
24. They have ____ in the way of Cain. (Jude 11)
25. Aaron the ____ of the LORD. (Ps. 106:16)
28. Thou wilt not leave my soul in ____. (Acts 2:27)
29. He that acknowledgeth the Son hath the Father ____. (1 John 2:23)
30. Sin, taking occasion by the commandment, deceived me, and by it ____ me. (Rom. 7:11)
32. Moneyless trades.
33. Scoffers, ____ after their own lusts. (2 Peter 3:3)
35. The Philistines, and smote them, until they came under Beth-____. (1 Sam. 7:11)
36. The same also that ascended up ____ above all heavens. (Eph. 4:10)
37. His meat was locusts and wild ____. (Matt. 3:4)
39. Though I be ____ in speech. (2 Cor. 11:6)
40. Epic poetry.
41. Agrippa was come, and Bernice, with great ____. (Acts 25:23)
42. Sent forth the Spirit of his Son into your hearts, crying, ____, Father. (Gal. 4:6)
45. Whose mouth must be held in with ____ and bridle. (Ps. 32:9)
47. And all were baptized unto Moses in the cloud and in the ____. (1 Cor. 10:2)
48. Just ____, vexed with the filthy conversation. (2 Peter 2:7)
49. Direction: Nazareth to Tiberias.

Answers

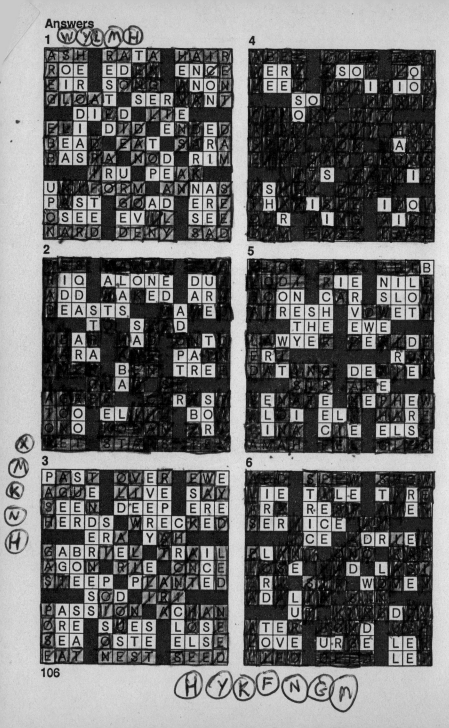

7

AIDE
NTE DED
WEE SAD

A
CRE
E W
MDA

A
RE ERE
EE RAN ETTA

10

EA DEA DL
AT MMANDE
STEA EAR

EW EE
SA D D ASD
ARA TA SLO
PE T T E
R DW
DA ANT READ
SA PEAR DA
R L NT ARO

8

S AREG E
ER TEND N E
R SED SD
H D E

ASE E
IEN N
NS N

N
FE DO
SEE REE E

11

RI VE LEA
E E ISL
AR DRY PE
HE E
RA ST
E EE
E E
DO E
P Y MER
CHE EVE
RTS EKER DE

9

VINCE EDISON
O XEN SIN W
EL SCOTT S
EV L ERE LONG
ED RANGE
STUNNED
RITING A
ERS LEG NAME
A TESLA TON
E AR ARE
RIKAS SERENE
ERAPH

12

E A R YEA
ER E RAR
I NE
SX TIR
PE T LE
I P I
NE I
E E T
T E
AR RE TURE
IN E SEE

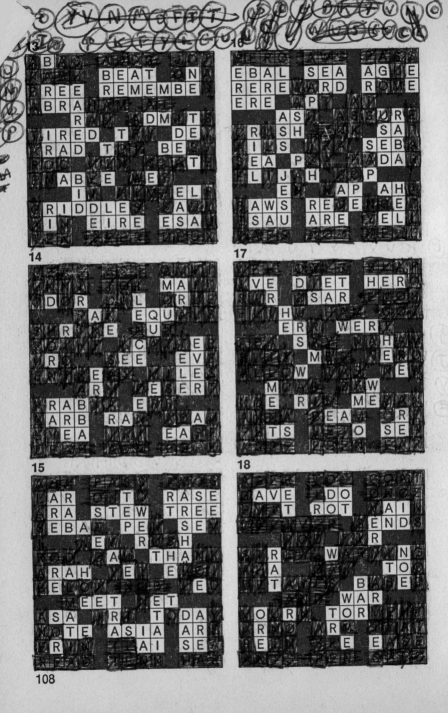

108

19

EASE
A E
SLE EED
SPS WEN
PEY D
PES E
EN BA WEL
T
U SE
D T KE ST
E GEE

22

AL ALA RA
N ANT
HE L LE
RE RED
T R A
RAL R L
SARA E
AR RE
L ERE
EE RA IN
A EDEN ERA

20

CAMP NEED
AHIR AREA PAD
P A
BAND TE
R
O P TE
P
E
P E
I E OK
RR OE RGE
EE TEE EE

23

B
M RIPE AW
MI INSTA LE
SSES N
T ANGE
LEA RET RA
BBE A
SE S NEW
RE TS E
APPA
ASTREAT
ARE ELSE EKE

21

WEB STEW T
E E THEE R
SET RENT VOT
TR ERS SORES
EWE
PANTS ST PES
E TR
ENS E
TS
B
RA R
EI
DA ES R

24

RE FEAR ONE
A E RE AT
SMEL ED AHO
T ND SH SA
AG P SAR
ND DE HAGA
BE HE
ALES SARDINE
RE ESA ADA
SEE REAL LEA

109

KWYCD

25

```
MASS  ASS  ALSO
ABLE  WAH  SAAB
REIN  AMY  LINE
ATTACK   ENERGY
     TOE  LOE
TAVERN   DEPART
AGE        NIT
JOTHAM   LISTEN
     ADO  ASP
CARPET   SHINED
LEAP  HIT  NINE
URGE  ERE  ELON
BIEN  RID  SESS
```

28

```
HABA  AMT  PEAS
ACER  HOE  RABA
THEE  ARM  ESEK
HENNA  APOSTLE
      AD  LOVE
SIA  VIS  ENSUE
AFRAID   ARTIST
DEEDS  ERR  SEE
     MESS  AH
CHRISTS   NIGHT
HOAR  RED  ROAR
AMIE  ANI  ANNE
REND  WEN  MEDE
```

26

```
COMA  PLEB  EVE
ASER  RAMA  DIN
RENO  ATIP  END
BEAUTY  STONES
    HSH  ASIN
TREE  PRIZE  AN
RIM  THROE  AGO
YE  RAYON  EBER
    ENSW  OAR
JEHUDI  STRAWS
ADO  ECCL  THAT
DOR  MAUI  HADE
AMI  SLED  YMIR
```

29

```
ASA  AIDE  CHOP
MAD  CLAN  LAME
APOSTLES  OREN
    AS  MUSTARD
ARMY  DOETH
RIE  BON  AESOP
MOTHER  ANSELM
STEEL  END  AET
    ALOUD  AMOS
LANTERN  EM
ARAH  DISCIPLE
MADE  ECHO  AIR
ADAN  REEL  SEE
```

27

```
SALA  ASS  DARE
ALAS  LOP  ORAN
STOP  WOODLAND
HOSEA  TOIL
    CLE  FRAMED
STATION  TRADE
WAR  NOW  REB
AMISS  SERVANT
YELLOW  BEE
    ORAL  DRANE
SHOWERED  IRON
TIRE  TAR  LEAD
SPED  SHY  YAHS
```

30

```
TREE  CRY  BOTH
HARA  RUE  ASEA
EBER  USA  SENT
    WHET  SHETH
DAMIEL  THE
OMEGA  THYSELF
RIT  ICY  LIE
MESSIAH  HOSEA
    INN  PARENT
STALK  NAME
HOME  MOP  GIFT
OMEN  ARE  IRAE
WENT  WAR  MINE
```

31

```
I S H   P A N S   S E T A
D O E   O S E E   I R O N
O I L   U P O N   G R E Y
L E P E R   N E A H
      L E D   H E E D E D
W A Y   D I M   S T O N E
A R E A   E A R   H E A R
R E A P S   D E W   R N A
S T R O D E   D I N
      S A L T   N O B L E
W E S T   D E A N   R O D
E V I L   E L S E   E V E
T I R E   R E A D   D E N
```

34

```
A R T S   J O B   S H E M
L O R E   E V E   H O V E
A D A R   R E D   E W E S
S A V I O U R   W E L T S
    E A U S   B A T
T E L L T A L E S   W A S
A Y E S   L E T   E R N E
R E D   B E T H S A I D A
      H I M   L A S T
S H O O T   R E P E A T S
H O A R   H A H   F B O A
E R R S   A T E   U L N A
W I S E   S E M   L E E R
```

32

```
A R A B   E V I L   S O W
P A C E   L I N E   A W E
E P H E S I A N S   L E T
S E E   H A L   S I T
      M O B   S O N   H O
A H E A D   D A N   B A N
B O R N   N E W   G A V E
E L I   T O W   C A R E S
L E   S A T   T O P
      R O B   O W L   A R A
A R E   L E V I T I C U S
S U E   E V E N   S N I P
A N D   S I N S   H E N S
```

35

```
E N D   S U S A   G R A B
P A R   K N O W   R A C A
I C E   A D U L T E R E R
C H A T T E R   R E E D S
      D O E R   S I N
W A F T S   H E M   D O E
A G U E   S O W   W E R E
S O L   O A R   M I S E R
      A P T   M I N T
A D O R E   P I L G R I M
S E V E N F O L D   O N O
O P E N   P O L E   Y E T
R A R A   S L O W   S E E
```

33

```
H A D   M O T E   T H A N
A R E   E V I L   H U G E
S A P   D E L I V E R E R
    A D A R   I S L E
A A R O N   W A N E
S I T E   R I B E   G R R
E N E   T I D E S   L E E
R E D   I D O L   S E A L
      F L E W   R E A D Y
  F R E E   S E E N
P L E A S U R E S   I R A
S E E S   R A N T   N O R
F E L T   E N D S   G E T
```

36

```
A R A B   D A M   I N G S
H A I R   I R A   N E R O
S T R I N G E D   S A I L
      N E S   T U R N S
L O D G E   B A A L
E N O S   L E N G T H E N
A T E   L O G O S   A P O
F O R G I V E N   A T E R
      L A E T   O S H E A
L I V E R   I N K
I D E A   R E D E E M E R
M O R N   A W E   S A V E
A L A S   S E A   T R E E
```

37

```
I L L S   L E V I   R A N
R E A P   E V E N   E R E
K A N A   P A T S   D E W
S H A R P E N   U S E
      T A R   F R E E S T
M E D A N   S E E   M A R
A D A N   H E N   M E R E
M E N   P I T   V E R S E
A N G E L S   H A S
    L E E   M E S S I A S
E L I   A R A M   A M M I
W O N   S A R A   G L A D
E G G   E B E N   E A S E
```

40

```
D R A W   A G E S   A G O
R A R A   I R A N   M O B
A P E S   R A G E   O R E
G E   T D   B L E S S E D
    P E O R   E R E
A M I   G A D   S L E E P
S E L F   W E B   L A T E
S T E A L   W A S   R A N
    T O I   D I G S
T H R E A T S   A I   A H
R U E   N A L A   A B L E
U S E   E L O N   N A I L
E E L   D Y E D   T R I P
```

38

```
W A R S   L E A F   A H A
A L A T   A N T E   D A N
S E V E N T E E N   A R T
P E E W E E   C O M E S
    A T   S E E N
O D E R   H A R D   T O O
F O N D   A R I   B A N I
F E D   E R A N   A B E L
    I L A I   A Z
N A O M I   F E A S T S
I N N   J E R U S A L E M
N O E   A R A N   R A T E
E N S   H I N D   S P E W
```

41

```
M A S S   T I E D   I R A
A M Y T   R O V E   L A C
R I C O   A N E T   A C T
    A R T   A N A N I A S
R I M M E D   T I E
A G O   N E T   N A H A M
M A R A   N O T   H E R A
A L E R T   P A W   R O I
    A R E   R E N O W N
A N I M A L S   B A D
M I D   D I A L   G I A H
O N E   E A V E   G A L A
S E A   S H E D   E S P Y
```

39

```
L O T S   R A C E   L O T
E A S T   I R R A   O N E
S T A R   S O O T   A T E
S H R A N K   W I S D O M
    Y O I   N N E
A L L   E N E   G L A S S
S E E N   G A L   F I A T
H E R O D   R I B   R Y E
    A R T   T E E
M O T H E R   H E L P E D
A M I   A I D E   D A R E
R A M   M A I L   E L S E
A R E   S L E Y   R E E D
```

42

```
H E L P   S L Y   S P A N
I L E O   T O E   P A G E
L I A R   A I N   A R E A
L A N T E R N   M I T E R
    I R E   L E N A
L A B O R   S O N   K O R
I R O N   S E T   M E N E
P T A   H A M   H E R O D
    S P E D   S I R
W A T E R   W A T C H E S
A R E T   B E L   I A L U
R I R E   A R M   E A S E
M A S S   Y E A   S K A T
```

43

A	S	K	S		T	R	A		D	I	E	S
D	U	E	T		W	A	S		E	S	A	U
D	E	A	R		I	N	K		B	U	R	N
			E	O	N				T	I	N	S
H	A	D	A	R		O	I	D	O			
A	H	E	M		I	S	C	A	R	I	O	T
R	I	E		A	L	I	E	N		D	A	H
E	S	P	O	U	S	E	D		S	I	R	E
			R	E	A	R		T	H	O	S	E
M	A	L	A				R	O	I			
O	N	A	N		A	D	O		N	E	W	S
C	O	N	G		R	I	M		E	V	E	N
K	N	E	E		T	E	E		D	E	N	Y

46

A	G	E	S		R	A	G	E		T	R	Y
M	A	R	A		A	R	A	D		H	O	E
I	T	E	M		H	A	D		D	E	B	T
D	E		A	H	A	B		H	E			
		C	R	I	B		R	E	W	A	R	D
C	L	A	I	M		O	A	R		L	A	Y
L	A	R	A		S	U	N		A	P	S	E
A	D	O		S	I	T		A	B	H	O	R
P	E	N	N	E	R		A	R	R	A		
			A	M		A	R	E	A		A	S
D	A	M	P		O	R	E		H	A	L	O
A	G	E		O	N	A	N		A	D	A	N
N	O	T		R	A	M	A		M	E	S	S

44

R	A	N	G		A	H	S		D	O	G	S
A	M	I	R		S	E	T		E	V	I	L
M	A	L	E		A	R	A		S	I	D	E
S	L	E	E	P		B	R	A	I	D	E	D
			T	A	R		S	I	R			
W	O	R	S	H	I	P		R	E	E	D	S
O	U	T		B	A	T		H	E	A		
T	R	E	E	S		W	I	L	L	I	N	G
			P	O	T		P	A	I			
W	I	T	H	O	U	T		D	A	V	I	D
E	D	E	R		B	A	G		B	A	R	E
N	E	R	O		A	R	E		L	I	A	R
D	A	M	N		L	O	T		E	N	D	S

45

H	A	D		M	E	R	E		T	H	A	N
A	R	E		E	V	I	L		H	U	G	E
S	A	P		D	E	L	I	V	E	R	E	R
			A	D	A	N		I	S	L	E	
A	A	R	O	N		W	I	N	E			
S	I	T	E		W	I	S	E		P	H	R
E	N	E		T	I	D	E	S		L	E	E
R	E	D		I	D	O	L		S	E	A	L
			F	L	E	W		R	E	A	D	Y
	F	R	E	E			S	E	E	D		
P	L	E	A	S	U	R	E	S		I	R	A
S	E	E	S		S	E	N	T		N	O	R
T	A	F	T		E	N	D	S		G	E	T

48

H	A	R		T	A	L	L		S	I	T	A
A	G	E		O	L	E	O		E	N	O	S
R	A	M		W	O	N	T		N	I	N	E
P	R	E	T	E	N	D		W	A	T	E	R
			M	O	R	E		B	A	T		
A	B	B	E	S		D	E	S	E	R	T	S
S	U	E		B	A	D			E	W	E	
A	B	R	A	H	A	M		G	A	V	O	T
			T	A	R		S	O	L	E		
C	H	A	R	M		V	I	O	L	A	T	E
H	E	R	O		W	I	L	D		L	A	D
A	R	E	T		O	V	A	L		E	R	E
Y	E	A	H		E	A	S	Y		D	E	N

113

49

A	M	M	I		P	R	E		A	R	O	D
S	E	E	N		A	I	R		R	O	W	Y
E	R	O	S		S	C	R	A	M	B	L	E
R	E	S	T	A	T	E		C	O			
			E	R	E		C	H	R	I	S	T
C	H	E	A	T		L	I	E		J	A	R
H	E	R	D		C	E	S		T	O	M	E
A	R	M		A	R	E		C	O	N	E	Y
R	E	A	L	L	Y		H	O	N			
			I	S		M	E	S	S	I	A	H
D	I	S	C	O	V	E	R		U	R	G	E
E	S	E	K		O	N	O		R	O	E	S
W	E	T	S		W	E	D		E	N	D	S

50

M	O	A	B		A	S	K		T	R	A	P
E	R	I	E		D	O	E		H	E	R	E
T	E	N	T		A	W	E		O	N	T	O
			H	A	M		P	A	S	T	O	R
H	A	G	A	R		S	I	R	E			
A	L	O	N	E		A	N	T		H	A	S
M	A	N	Y		B	I	G		W	E	L	L
I	S	E		C	A	N		F	A	L	S	E
			H	A	R	T		A	L	L	O	W
R	E	P	O	R	T		A	R	K			
U	P	O	N		E	B	B		I	S	L	E
D	O	M	E		R	I	B		N	E	O	N
E	S	P	Y		S	T	A		G	A	T	E